Houghton Mifflin
English

Shirley Haley-James   **John Warren Stewig**

Marcus T. Ballenger   Jacqueline L. Chaparro   Nancy C. Millett
June Grant Shane   C. Ann Terry

HOUGHTON   MIFFLIN   COMPANY   BOSTON

Atlanta   Dallas   Geneva, Illinois   Palo Alto   Princeton   Toronto

W9-BQW-860

Acknowledgments

The publisher has made every effort to locate each owner of the copyrighted material reprinted here. Any information enabling the publisher to rectify or credit any reference is welcome.

The Bear's Toothache by David McPhail. Copyright © 1972 by David McPhail. By permission of Little, Brown and Company in association with The Atlantic Monthly Press.

The Forgetful Bears by Lawrence Weinberg. Illustration copyright © 1981 by Paula Winter. Reprinted by permission of Scholastic, Inc.

"The Letter" from *Frog and Toad Are Friends* by Arnold Lobel. Copyright © 1970 by Arnold Lobel. Reprinted by permission of Harper & Row, Publishers, Inc., and William Heinemann Limited.

"Lost in the Museum," from *Lost in the Museum* by Miriam Cohen, illustrations by Lillian Hoban. Illustrations copyright © 1979 by Lillian Hoban. By permission of Greenwillow Books (A Division of William Morrow & Co.).

"Lunch for a Dinosaur," by Bobbi Katz from the poem "Company" in *Upside Down and Inside Out: Poems for All Your Pockets*, published by Franklin Watts, Inc. Copyright © 1973 by Bobbi Katz. Reprinted by permission of the author.

Mike Mulligan and His Steam Shovel by Virginia Lee Burton. Copyright 1939 and © 1967 by Virginia Lee Demetrios. Reprinted by permission of Houghton Mifflin Company.

"Move Over," from *Little Raccoon and Poems from the Woods* by Lilian Moore. Copyright © 1975 by Lilian Moore. Reprinted by permission of Marian Reiner for the author.

"The Owl," from *Zoo Doings* by Jack Prelutsky. Copyright © 1967, 1983 by Jack Prelutsky. By permission of Greenwillow Books (A Division of William Morrow & Company).

"The Pickety Fence," from *Every Time I Climb a Tree* by David McCord. Copyright 1952, © 1972 by David McCord. By permission of Little, Brown and Company, and George Harrap, Ltd.

Credits

Illustrations

Meg Kelleher Aubrey: 85, 86, 89, 91, 121, 123, 161, 171, 211, 233 (borders): 81, 82, 113, 114, 117, 118, 158, 199, 219
Virginia Lee Burton: 22, 23, 24
Christine Czernotta: 72, 160, 164, 165, 168, 212, 228, 230
Robert Daemmrich: 10
Laura Ferraro: 127
Lillian Hoban: 96
Susan Lexa: 25, 27, 28, 29, 45, 46, 47, 55, 56, 57, 58, 71, 73, 74, 75, 76, 79, 80, 82, 104, 107, 109, 110, 117, 125, 156, 158, 163, 167, 189, 190, 195, 196, 199, 200, 203, 204, 207, 208, 213, 227, 232, 235, 244, 245, 246, 247, 248, 249, 250, 251, 252, 253, 254, *Opposites Games, Naming Word Game*
Arnold Lobel: 128
Jane McCreary: 31, 32, 33, 34, 35, 43, 44, 49, 50, 51, 52, 77, 78, 81, 103, 111, 112, 126, 127, 129, 130, 131, 143, 144, 151, 152, 154, 156, 169, 170, 175, 176, 191, 192, 193, 194, 216, 223, 224
David McPhail: 19, 20
Paul Sances: 90, 92, 108, 119, 120, 124, 129, 162, 166, 227, 229 (borders) 82, 113, 114, 158, 204, 224
Carol Schwartz: 173, 174, 175, 176 (borders)
Ann Schweninger: 95, 96 (borders)
George Ulrich: 87, 88, 93, 118, 122, 209, 210, 231
Lou Vaccaro: 1, 11–16, 21, 39, 41, 42, 63–68, 72, 105, 106, 139, 145–150, 153, 155, 157, 159, 177, 201, 202, 215, 217, 218, 220, 221, 222, 225, 229, 241, 242, 243, *Rhyme Game, Number Word Game, Sentence Game, Describing Word Game*
Joe Veno: (borders) 6, 7, 11–16, 25, 36, 98, 132, 133, 157, 177, 178, 179, 238
Paula Winter: 236

Photographs

10 Peter Fronk/Click/Chicago. **18** Daemmrich. **29** Michal Heron. **30** Kim Massie/Rainbow. **38** Ulrike Welsch. **54** Allen Green/Photo Researchers Inc. **70** James H. Simon/The Picture Cube. **94** Daemmrich. **102** Elwin Williamson/The Picture Cube. **126** Cezus/Click/Chicago. **142** Daemmrich. **172** Jane Burton/Bruce Coleman Inc. **188** Bill Binzen. **198** (left) The Image Bank. **198** (right) Chuck Fishman/Woodfin Camp & Assoc. **214** Frank Siteman/The Picture Cube. **234** Jeff Reed/The Stock Shop.

Victoria Beller-Smith: 17, 37, 40, 53, 97, 99–101, 114, 134, 141, 184, 187, 198

Cover Photographs

Cover and title page photograph: Marcella Pedone/Image Bank

The photograph shows a garden in Piedmont, a northern region of Italy.

Back cover: Jon Chomitz

Table of Contents

Student's Handbook

Punchouts

Games

The Rhyme Game

The Color Game

The Number Word Game

The Opposites Game

The Sentence Game

The Naming Word Game

The Describing Word Game

Book Covers

My Book About Me

My Book of Favorites

My Story

Readiness
My Book About Me

Name

1 A Picture of Me

My name is

Children draw pictures of themselves, using the steps
of the writing process.

Unit 1: My Book About Me **11**

READINESS

2 | Where I Live

Unit 1: My Book About Me

Children draw pictures of their homes, using the steps of the writing process.

WRITING PROCESS READINESS

3 | My Family

Children draw pictures of their families, using the
steps of the writing process.

Unit 1: My Book About Me

Name _____

4 | My Best Friends

Children draw pictures of their best friends, using the steps of the writing process.

WRITING PROCESS READINESS

5 | My School

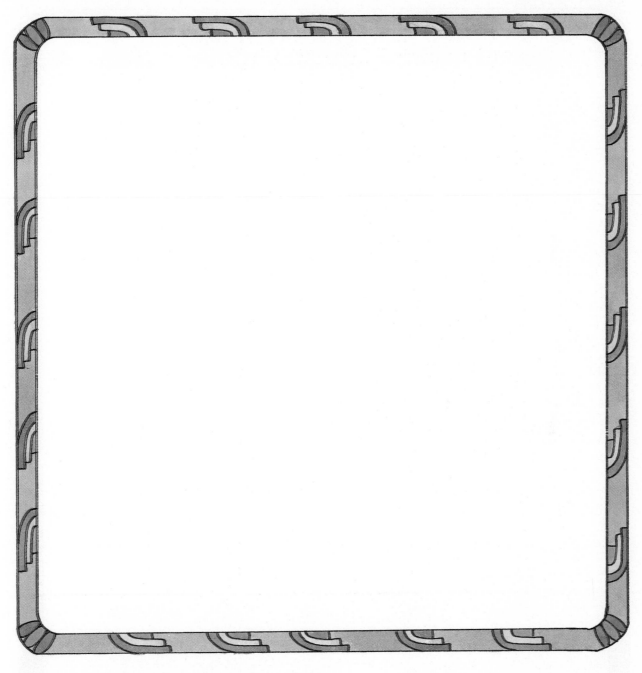

The name of my school is

_____

- -

_____ •

Children draw pictures of their school, using the steps of the writing process.

Name

WRITING PROCESS READINESS

6 | When I Grow Up

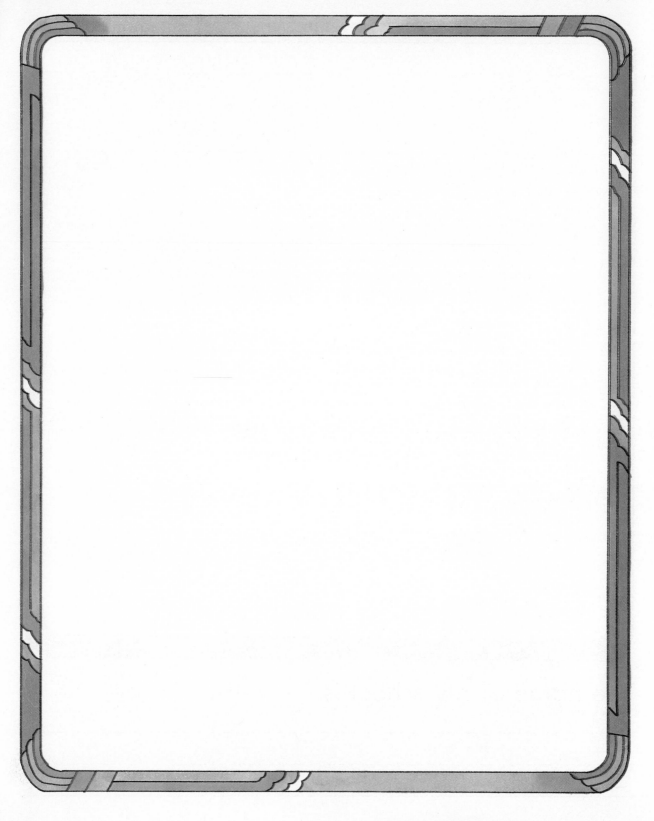

16   **Unit 1: My Book About Me**

Children draw pictures of what they want to be when they grow up, using the steps of the writing process.

7 | Making My Book

Children make books of their finished drawings,
using the covers provided at the back of the book.

Unit 1: My Book About Me   17

Readiness
Listening and Speaking

Name _____

LISTENING

 1 ‖ Listening for Details

Listen and look.

The Bear's Toothache
by DAVID MCPHAIL

Children listen to a story, discuss illustrations, and
recall details from the story.

Listening for Details continued

Remember and draw.

Children recall and draw an incident from the story.

Name

LISTENING

2 Listening for Rhyme

 Listen and match.

Children listen to a poem and match pictures
illustrating rhyming words from the poem.

Unit 2: Listening and Speaking   21

Listen and look.

Mike Mulligan and His Steam Shovel

by VIRGINIA LEE BURTON

Children listen to a story and look at pictures
showing the sequence of events.

Listening for Sequence continued

Children listen to a story and look at pictures showing the sequence of events.

Unit 2: Listening and Speaking

Listening for Sequence continued

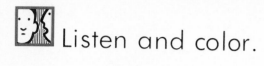 Listen and color.

Children order pictures in the correct sequence.

Name

SPEAKING

4 | Telling a Story

Look and discuss.

1.

2.

3.
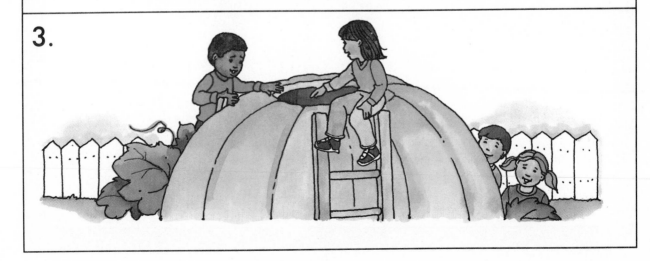

Children discuss pictures and tell a story to go
along with them.

Unit 2: Listening and Speaking   25

Telling a Story continued

Draw and color.

Children draw a picture illustrating an outcome of the story.

SPEAKING

5 | Talking About Taking Turns

 Discuss and mark.

 Draw and color.

Children discuss, mark, and draw pictures.

SPEAKING

6 | Talking Without Words

Discuss and match.

1.

2.

3.

Children match situations and gestures.

SPEAKING

7 | Answering the Phone

Listen and mark.

1.

2.

3.

Children mark pictures to answer questions about a telephone conversation.

Name

1 ║ My Favorite Toy

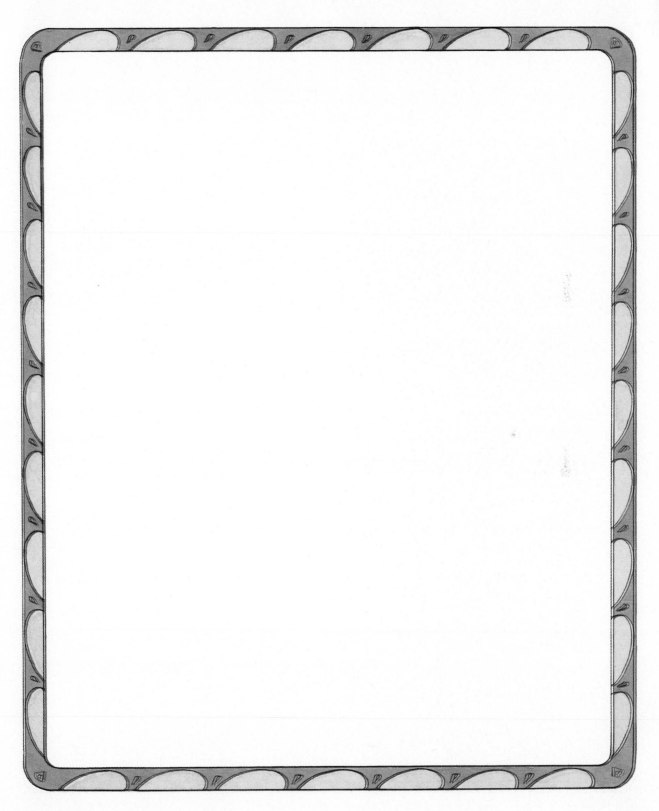

Children draw pictures of their favorite toys, using the steps of the writing process.

Unit 3: My Book of Favorites

2 | My Favorite Food

Unit 3: My Book of Favorites

Children draw pictures of their favorite foods, using the steps of the writing process.

WRITING PROCESS READINESS

3 | My Favorite Animal

Children draw pictures of their favorite animals,
using the steps of the writing process.

READINESS

WRITING PROCESS READINESS

4 | My Favorite Place

Unit 3: My Book of Favorites

Children draw pictures of their favorite places, using the steps of the writing process.

WRITING PROCESS READINESS

5 | My Favorite Storybook Character

Children draw pictures of their favorite storybook characters, using the steps of the writing process.

Unit 3: My Book of Favorites 35

Name

WRITING PROCESS READINESS

6 | What I Like to Do Best

36 Unit 3: My Book of Favorites

Children draw pictures of what they like to do, using the steps of the writing process.

Name _____

7 Making My Book

Children make books of their finished drawings,
using the covers provided at the back of the book.
They share their finished work.

Unit 3: My Book of Favorites 37

Readiness
Listening and Thinking

LISTENING

1 | Following Directions

Listen and mark.

1. ✗			

2. —			

3. 0			

Children listen to and follow one-step directions.

Unit 4: Listening and Thinking 39

Following Directions continued

Listen and make.

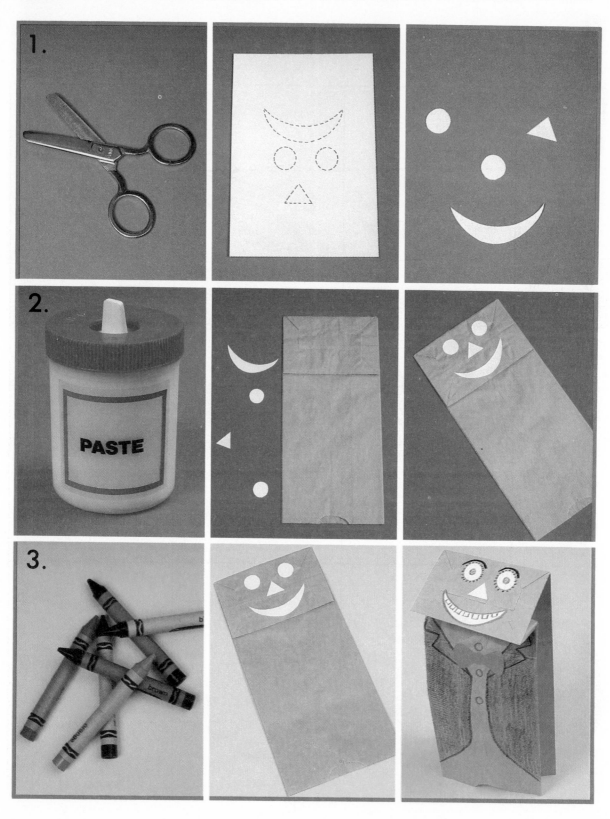

Unit 4: Listening and Thinking

Children listen to and follow three-step directions.

Name _____

LISTENING

2 | Colors

 Listen and color.

Children listen and color a picture according to teacher's directions.

Unit 4: Listening and Thinking

41

Colors continued

Look and color.

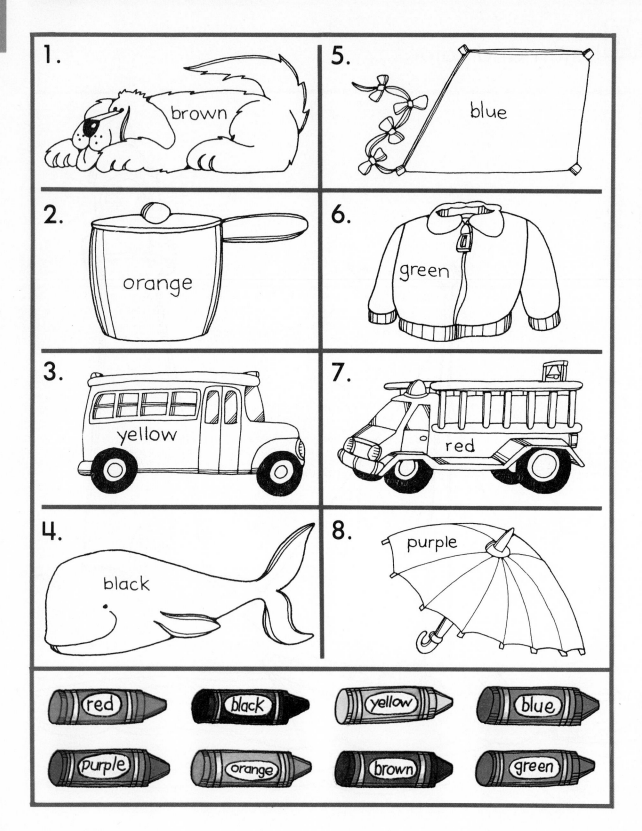

1. brown

2. orange

3. yellow

4. black

5. blue

6. green

7. red

8. purple

red   black   yellow   blue

purple   orange   brown   green

Children color pictures according to teacher's directions.

Name

LISTENING

3 up, down, in, out

Listen and color.

Children listen to directions and color people
and objects that are up, down, in, and out.

Unit 4: Listening and Thinking 43

Name

4 | Top, Middle, Bottom

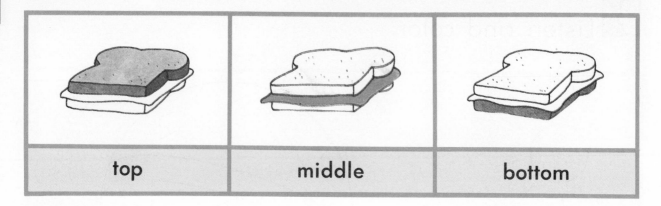

| top | middle | bottom |

Listen and color.

1.

2.

3.

4.

Children listen to directions and color objects in the top, middle, or bottom position.

LISTENING

5 | Left and Right

Listen and color.

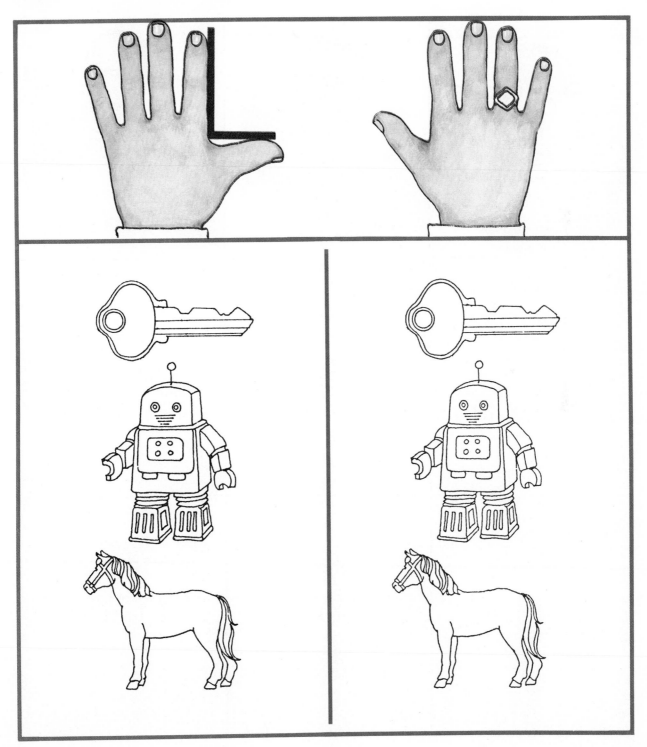

Children listen to directions and color objects on their
left-hand and right-hand sides.

Unit 4: Listening and Thinking   45

Name

THINKING

6 | First, Next, Last

 Talk about the pictures.

| first | next | last |
| first | next | last |

Children discuss order words. Then they cut pictures from page 47 and paste them in correct sequence here.

First, Next, Last continued

 Cut and paste.

Children cut out these pictures and paste them in correct sequence on page 46.

Unit 4: Listening and Thinking

47

Name _____

THINKING

7 | Which Is Different?

 Look and mark.

Children mark the object in each row that is different.

Name

THINKING

8 | Matching Shapes

Look and color.

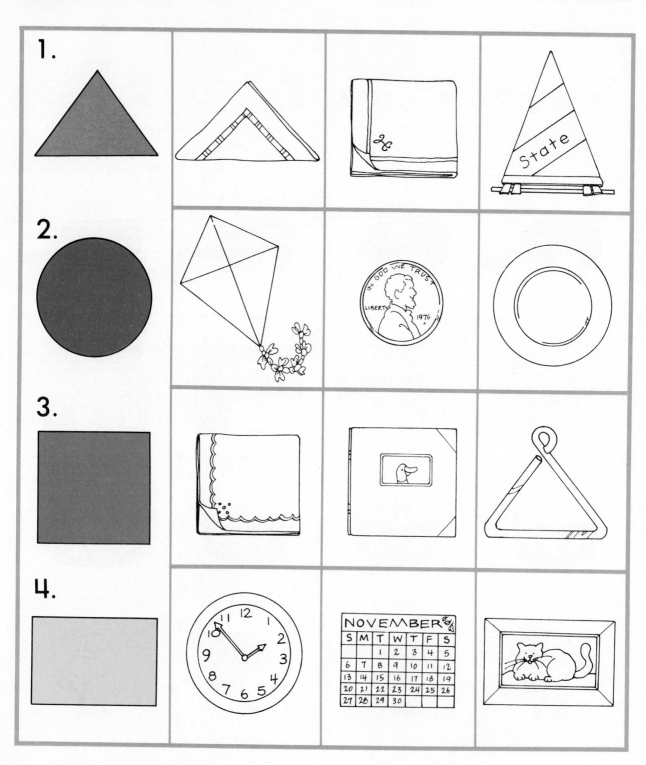

1.

2.

3.

4.

Unit 4: Listening and Thinking

Children color objects in each row that match the shape at the beginning of the row.

THINKING

9 | Grouping Objects

✏️ Look and match.

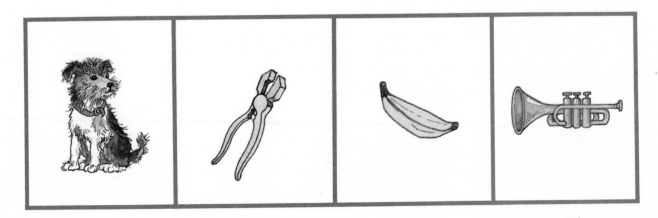

Children group objects by category.

Unit 4: Listening and Thinking 51

Grouping Objects continued

 Look and mark.

1.

2.

3.

4.

5.

52 **Unit 4: Listening and Thinking**

Children group objects by function.

THINKING

10 | Signs

Listen and mark.

Children follow directions to mark the correct signs.

Name

1 Tracing and Writing Letters

Look	Trace	Write

✏️ Trace and write each letter.

c c ☐ a a ☐ o o ☐

e e ☐ s s ☐

i i ☐ r r ☐

n n ☐ m m ☐

u u ☐ v v ☐ w w ☐

Children trace and write lower-case letters.

Unit 5: Letters and Numbers 55

Tracing and Writing Letters continued

Look   Trace   Write

Trace and write each letter.

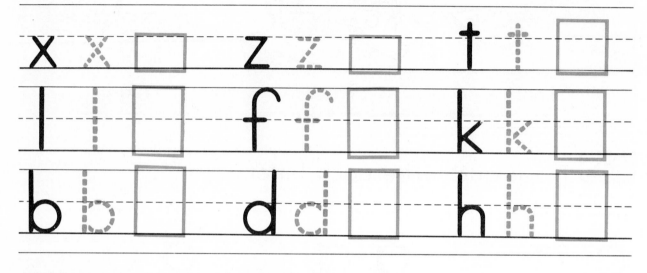

1. Write three letters that go below the bottom line.

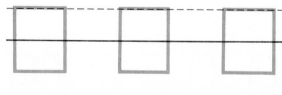

2. Write three letters that go above the dotted line.

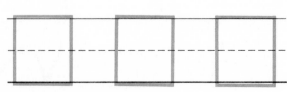

Children trace and write lower-case letters.

2 | Picture Clues

Name each picture. Trace and write
the letter that begins each picture name.

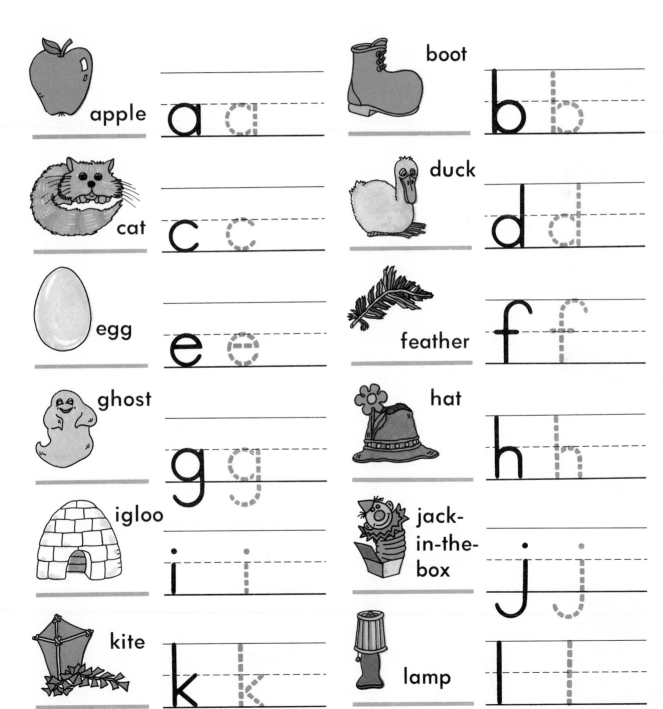

apple   a a

boot   b b

cat   c c

duck   d d

egg   e e

feather   f f

ghost   g g

hat   h h

igloo   i i

jack-in-the-box   j j

kite   k k

lamp   l l

Children trace and write lower-case letters.

Unit 5: Letters and Numbers

Trace and write the letter that begins each picture name.

monster

m m

nest

n n

octopus

o o

pig

p p

quarter

q q

rabbit

r r

sock

s s

tiger

t t

umbrella

u u

vest

v v

worm

w

x x

yo-yo

y y

zipper

z z

Children trace and write lower-case letters.

Name

3 | Writing Capital Letters in ABC Order

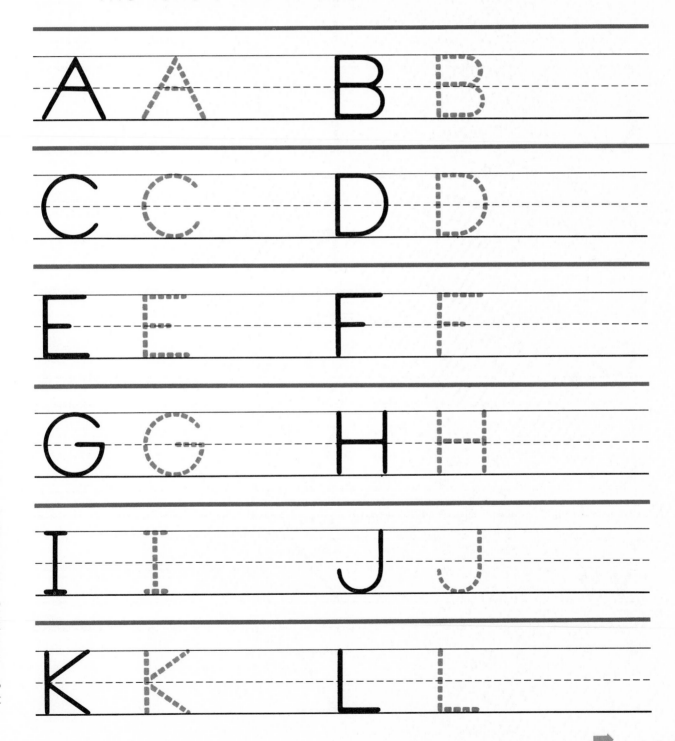 Trace and write each letter.
The letters are in ABC order.

Children trace and write capital letters.

Unit 5: Letters and Numbers 59

Writing Capital Letters in ABC Order continued

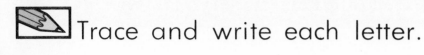Trace and write each letter.

M M N N

O O P P

Q Q R R

S S T T

U U V V

W W X X

Y Y Z Z

Unit 5: Letters and Numbers

Children trace and write capital letters.

Name _____

4 | Tracing and Writing My ABC's

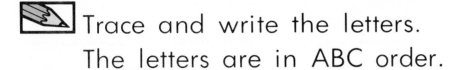 Trace and write the letters.
The letters are in ABC order.

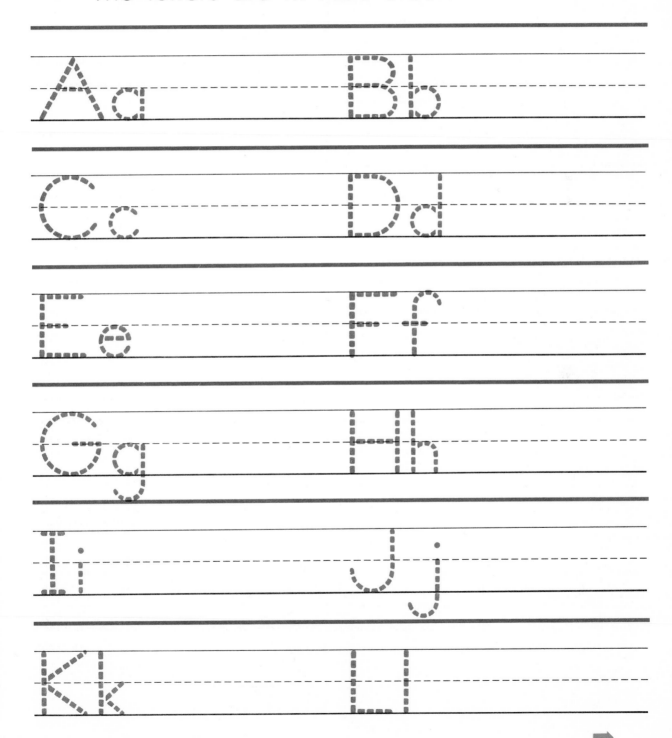

Children trace and write capital and
lower-case letters.

Unit 5: Letters and Numbers   **61**

Tracing and Writing My ABC's continued

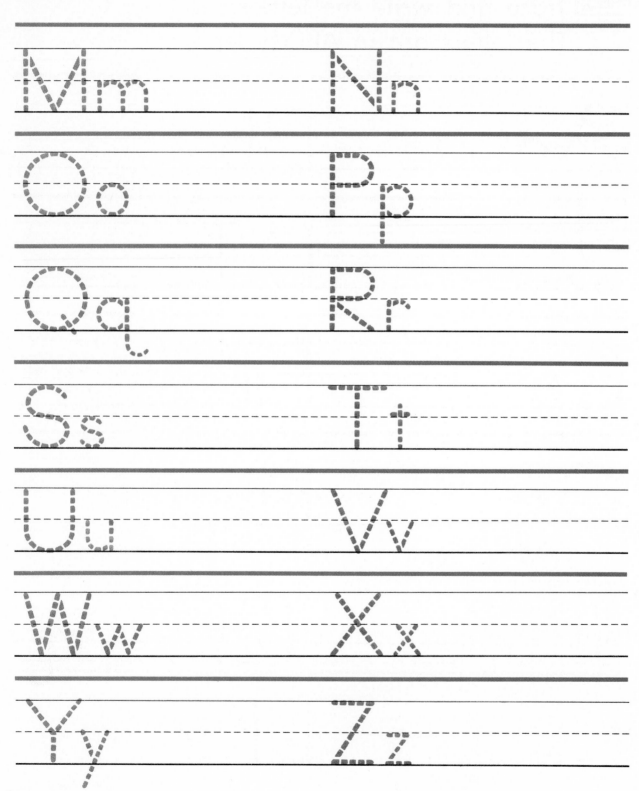Trace and write the letters.

Children trace and write capital and lower-case letters.

5 | ABC Order

These letters are in ABC order.
Write the missing letters.

A B C ☐ E F ☐

H I J ☐ ☐ L M ☐

O P Q R S T ☐

V W X ☐ ☐ Z

a b ☐ d e f ☐ h i

j ☐ l m n o ☐ q

r ☐ t u v ☐ ☐ x y z

Children write letters in ABC order.

Unit 5: Letters and Numbers

ABC Order continued

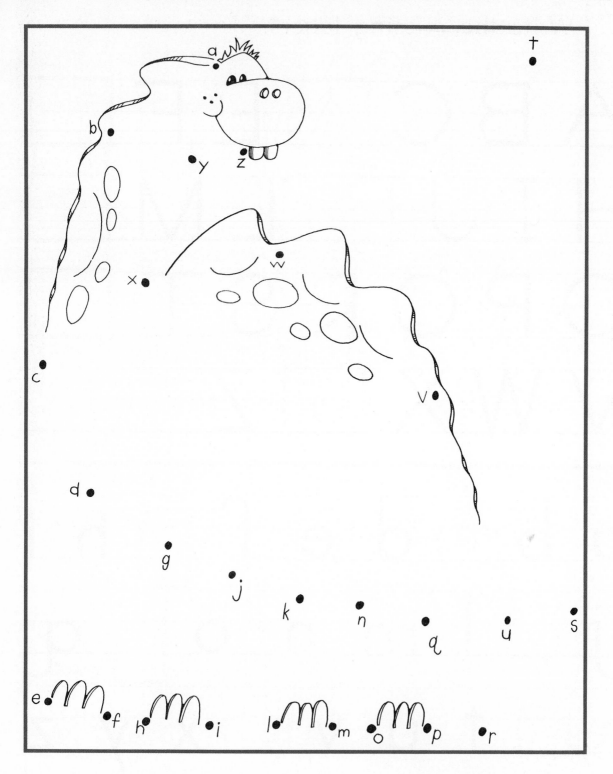

Draw a line from letter to letter.
Use ABC order. Color your picture.

Children connect the dots in ABC order.

6 | Tracing and Writing Numbers

Trace and write the numbers.

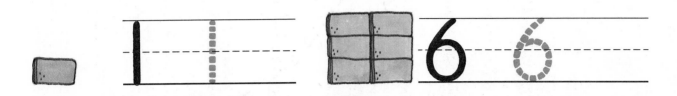

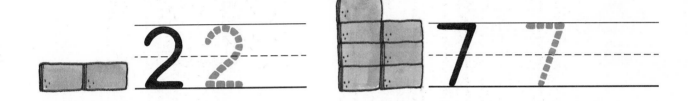

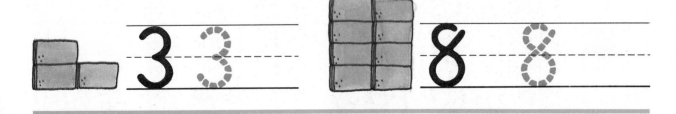

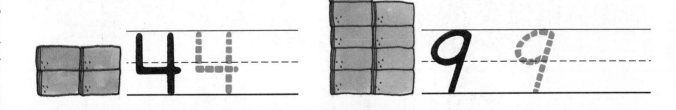

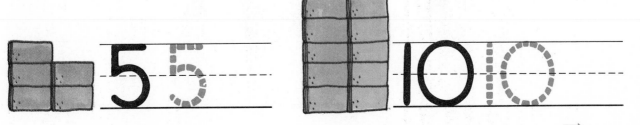

Children trace and write numerals.

Tracing and Writing **Numbers** continued

Trace the numbers. Then count the objects and write the correct number.

1 2 3 4 5 6 7 8 9 10

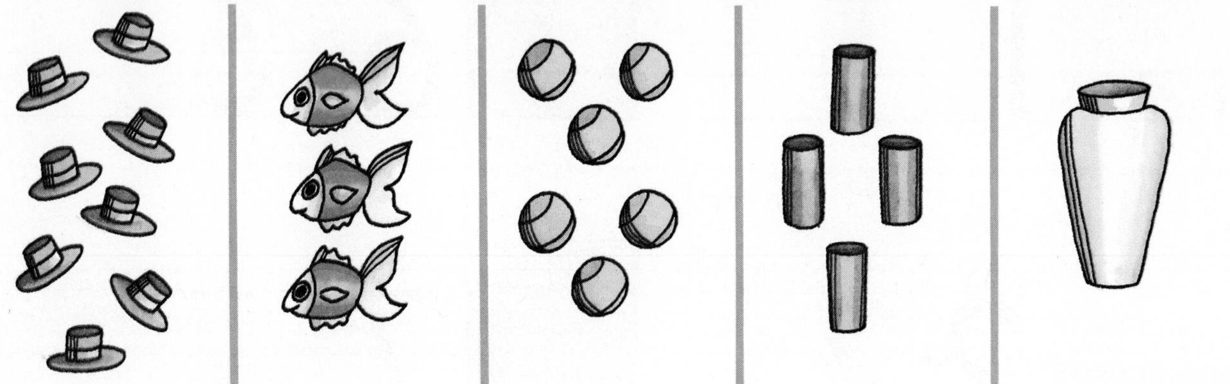

8

Unit 5: Letters and Numbers

Children count objects and trace and write numerals.

7 | Number Words

	1	one
	2	two

	3	three
	4	four

Trace each number word.
Draw pictures to show the number.

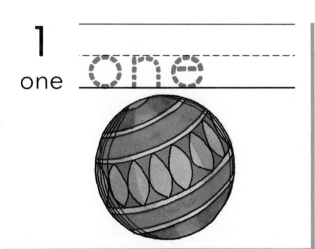

1
one

2
two

3
three

4
four

Children trace number words and draw an
equivalent number of objects.

Unit 5: Letters and Numbers 67

Number Words continued

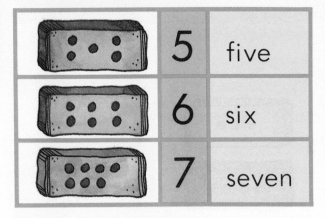

	5	five
	6	six
	7	seven

	8	eight
	9	nine
	10	ten

Trace each number word.
Draw pictures to show the number.

5
five

8
eight

6
six

9
nine

7
seven

10
ten

Children trace number words and draw an
equivalent number of objects.

8 | Phone Numbers I Need

 Write the names and phone numbers.

My number: _____

Parent's work:

Name _____

Number _____

Neighbor:

Name _____

Number _____

Children write important phone numbers.

Unit 5: Letters and Numbers

Language and Usage
Sentences

Name

Look at the picture. Tell about it.

Children use sentences to describe picture.
For Extra Practice, see p. 85.

2 | Naming Parts

Every sentence has two parts.
The **naming part** names someone or something.

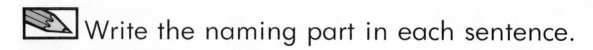 Write the naming part in each sentence.

Cows

1. _____ moo.

This dog

2. _____ barks.

A boy

3. _____ talks.

Match the sentence parts.

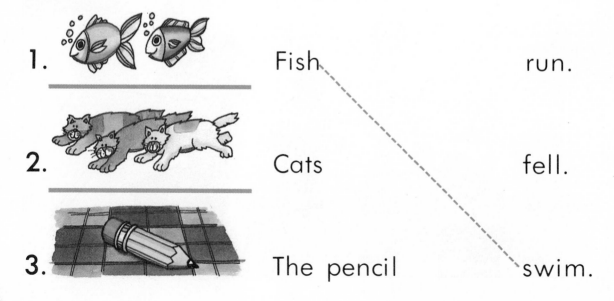

1. Fish   run.

2. Cats   fell.

3. The pencil   swim.

Children write and match naming parts (subjects).
For Extra Practice, see p. 86.

3 | Writing Naming Parts

Every sentence has a **naming part.**

Write a naming part for each sentence.

 **A duck**
 **The rabbit**
 **Mother**
 **Tom**
 **Kim**

1. Kim _____ hits the ball.

2. _____ swims in a lake.

3. _____ eats a plant.

4. _____ paints a picture.

5. _____ pats the dog.

Children write naming parts (subjects).
For Extra Practice, see p. 87.

4 | Action Parts

Every sentence has two parts.
The **action part** tells what someone or something does.

 Write the action part in each sentence.

jumps

1. The girl _____.

fell

2. Jill _____.

helped

3. Her friend _____.

 Match the sentence parts.

1. This bell   walks to school.

2. My cat   rings loudly.

3. Fred   sleeps all day.

Children write and match action parts (predicates).
For Extra Practice, see p. 88.

Name _____

Every sentence has an **action part.**

 Write an action part for each sentence.

1. Ducks __fly__.

2. Dad _____•

3. My sister _____•

4. Joey _____•

Children write action parts (predicates).
For Extra Practice, see p. 89.

Name _____

6 | Matching Sentence Parts

Naming Parts	Action Parts

✏️ Match naming parts and action parts.
Write the sentences.

1. My friend laughs.

2.

3.

Children write sentences.
For Extra Practice, see p. 90.

7 | Finding Sentence Parts

Every sentence has two parts.

Naming Parts	Action Parts

A frog | jumps.

My sister | walks to school.

✏️ Circle the naming parts.

1. (The cat) plays on the rug.

2. The cat plays with a ball.

3. Tabby hits the ball.

4. The ball rolls away.

5. This cat likes to play.

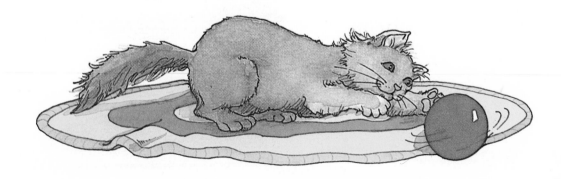

Children identify naming parts (subjects).

Finding Sentence Parts continued

Naming Part	Action Part
My cat	sleeps.

Draw a line under the action parts.

1. Children play in the park.

2. They swing on the swings.

3. The girls run to the lake.

4. The boys make boats.

Draw a line between the naming parts and the action parts.

1. The boy ┊ plays.

2. The cow eats hay.

3. Sue digs a hole.

Children identify naming parts (subjects) and action parts (predicates).
For Extra Practice, see p. 91.

8 | Which Is a Sentence?

Naming Part	Action Part
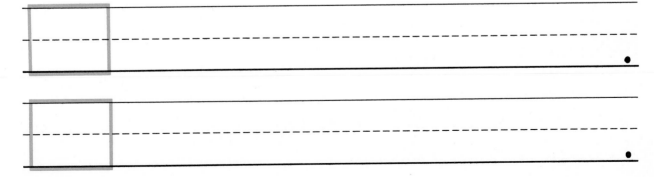	
Karen	threw the ball.

Read these word groups.
Write the two sentences.

1. the rabbit

2. The rabbit ran.

3. jumped up

4. She jumped up.

Children identify sentences.
For Extra Practice, see p. 92.

Name
_____

9 | Writing **I** in Sentences

Always write the word **I**
as a capital letter.

John and **I** read books.

 Write the word **I** in each sentence.

1. ____ love to read.

2. ____ like funny stories.

3. May ____ read your book?

4. Will ____ like it?

 Write a sentence with **I**.

_____

Children write the word **I** in sentences.
For Extra Practice, see p. 93.

Building Vocabulary

Opposites are words like **stop** and **go**.
The words **hot** and **cold** are also opposites.

 Write the word that belongs in
each sentence.

1. A rabbit is fast.  fast

A turtle is _slow._  slow

2. The tree is big.  big

The plant is _____ . small

3. The boy walks up. up

The girl walks _____ . down

4. The cat is in.  in

The dog is _____ .  out

Children write opposites.

Unit 6: Sentences 81

Name

Grammar-Writing Connection
Writing Sentences

Write a sentence for each picture.

Naming Part + Action Part

1. The girl swims.

2.

3.

4.

82   **Unit 6: Sentences**

Children write sentences.

Check-up: Unit 6

 Write a naming part for each sentence.

| Bobby |
| The bell |

1. ☐ _____ rings.

2. ☐ _____ plays ball.

 Write an action part for each sentence.

| counts |
| sleeps |
| sails |

1. The cat _____ .

2. The boy _____ .

3. The boat _____ .

 Write **I** to complete these sentences.

1. _____ found a key.   2. May _____ go?

Children review skills covered in Unit 6.

 Match sentence parts. Write the sentences.

Naming Parts		Action Parts	
The sun	Trees	grow tall.	shines.

1. ☐ _____ .

2. ☐ _____ .

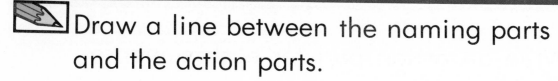 Draw a line between the naming parts and the action parts.

1. I look at a book.   3. My cat runs home.

2. The boat floats.   4. Cathy dances well.

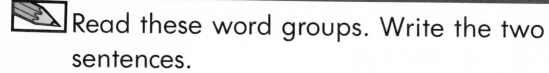 Read these word groups. Write the two sentences.

1. a fish   3. eats corn

2. A fish swims.   4. The hen eats corn.

1. ☐ _____ .

2. ☐ _____ .

Children review skills covered in Unit 6.

Extra Practice: Unit 6

1 || Speaking in Sentences

Look at the picture. Tell about it.

Now write a sentence about the picture.

_____

•

2 | Naming Parts

 Match each naming part with the picture.

● ▲

1.    Rain - - - - - - - - - - - -   grow.

2.    The plants   - - - - falls.

3.    The sun   plants seeds.

4.    Lee   shines.

 Look at the picture.
Write a sentence.

Children match naming parts (subjects) and write a sentence.

3 | Writing Naming Parts

 Write a naming part for each sentence.
● ▲

Pat

The dog

The bus

1. <u>The bus</u> stops outside.

2. ☐ _____ gets on the bus.

3. ☐ _____ wants to go too.

 Look at the pictures.
Write a sentence.
■

☐ _____ .

Children write naming parts (subjects) and a sentence.

● ▲ ■   **Three levels of practice**   87

Name

4 | Action Parts

 Match the sentence parts.
● ▲

1. This frog   buzz softly.

2. My cat   grew too big.

3. Bees   lives in a log.

4. This pig   sleeps in a hat.

 Look at the picture.
Write a sentence.

88   **Unit 6: Sentences**

Children match action parts (predicates) and write a sentence.

5 | Writing Action Parts

 Write an action part for each sentence.

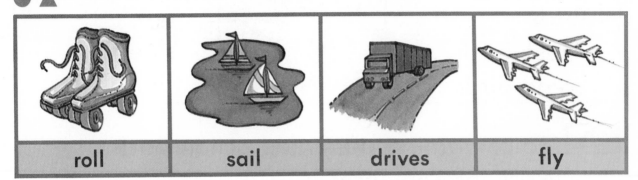

| roll | sail | drives | fly |

1. Roller skates  roll .

2. Boats _____ .

3. My mother _____ .

4. The planes _____ .

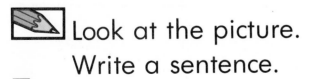 Look at the picture.
Write a sentence.

_____ .

Children write action parts (predicates) and a sentence.

● ▲ ■ **Three levels of practice**

6 | Matching Sentence Parts

Naming Parts		Action Parts
Birds		eat.
These birds		sleep.
Some birds		fly.

 Match naming parts and action parts.
Write the sentences.

● ▲

1.

2.

3.

 Look at the picture.
Write your own sentence.

■

Children write sentences.

Name _____

7 | Finding Sentence Parts

Naming Part	Action Part

The sun ⊃ ⊂ shines brightly.

✏️ Draw a line between the naming parts and the action parts.

●▲

1. The sun | sets slowly.

2. Light goes away.

3. The moon moves up in the sky.

4. A star winks at me.

5. Night has come.

✏️ Look at the picture. Write a sentence.

■

_____

- -

_____ •

Children identify naming parts (subjects) and action parts (predicates) and write a sentence.

● ▲ ■   **Three levels of practice**   **91**

8 | Which Is a Sentence?

Naming Part	Action Part
Harry	flew a kite.
The kite	sailed up.

Read these word groups.
Write the two sentences.

1. the string

3. ran home

2. The string broke.

4. Harry ran home.

Look at the picture.
Now write a sentence
of your own.

Children identify sentences and write a sentence.

9 | Writing I in Sentences

 Write the word **I** in each sentence.

1. **I** like to help.

2. Today ____ helped Mom and Dad.

3. ____ helped them paint.

4. Did ____ do a good job?

5. ____ think so!

 Draw a picture of yourself.
Write a sentence with **I**.

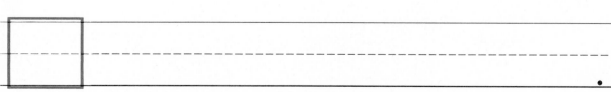

LITERATURE
Lunch for a Dinosaur
By Bobbi Katz

I'm fixing a lunch for a dinosaur.
Who knows when one might come by?
I'm pulling up all the weeds I can find.
I'm piling them high as the sky.
I'm fixing a lunch for a dinosaur.
I hope he will stop by soon.
Maybe he'll just walk down my street
And have some lunch at noon.

Lost in the Museum

By Miriam Cohen

THE WRITING PROCESS: DRAFTING

3 | Writing Our Story

This class wrote a story together.
Here is the story.

We made puppets. We used bags. We colored them. We had a show. Our parents came. They liked it.

Talk about your story.
Tell your teacher what you want to write.

Children discuss sample story and dictate a first
draft to teacher.

THE WRITING PROCESS: REVISING

4 | Writing More

The class talked about the story.
Then they wrote more.

We made ∧puppets. We used
        animal

paper
∧bags. We colored them.∧ We had
       We drew faces on them.

a show. Our parents came. They

liked it.

Read your class story together.
What do you want to add?

Children discuss sample class story and revise
their class story.

5 | Making a Final Copy

This is the final copy of the class story.

OUR CLASS STORY

Our Puppet Show

We made animal puppets. We used paper bags. We colored them. We drew faces on them. We had a show. Our parents came. They liked it.

 How can you show your class story?

Children discuss ways to display the final copy of their class story.

Language and Usage
More About Sentences

1 | Sentences Make Sense

A **sentence** makes sense. The words are in order.

me swims duck the to

(The duck swims to me.)

Circle the sentences.

The top is big.

1. is big top the

play to cats like

3. Cats like to play.

goes car the fast

2. The car goes fast.

A bird can fly.

4. can fly bird a

Children identify sentences.
For Extra Practice, see p. 117.

2 | Sentences Tell

Sentences that tell are **telling sentences.**

Draw a line under the telling sentence.

1. the boys   The boys play ball.

2. Two girls run.   girls two run

3. A girl sees ducks. A girl

4. the horse   The horse is big.

5. Annie and Jane   Annie and Jane play.

Children identify telling sentences.
For Extra Practice, see p. 118.

3 | Writing Capital Letters

A **telling sentence** begins with a **capital letter**.

This snake is long.

Begin each sentence with the word in the box.

Begin each sentence with a capital letter.

1. houses   Houses _____ have doors.

2. fish   _____ swim.

3. rabbits   _____ have tails.

4. balls   _____ are round.

5. grass   _____ is green.

Children capitalize the first words of sentences.
For Extra Practice, see p. 119.

Unit 8: More About Sentences   **105**

4 Writing Periods

A **telling sentence** ends with a **period.**

This train is long.

✏️ Put a period in the ○ at the end of
each sentence.

1. I like boats○

2. My friend likes boats○

3. Some boats are long○

4. My boat is red○

✏️ Copy each sentence. End it with a period.

1. I like cars

2. Jill likes boats

Children supply periods to end sentences.
For Extra Practice, see p. 120.

5 | Sentences Ask

Sentences that ask are **asking sentences.**

What is that?

How old is it?

Is it real?

Circle the asking sentences. Write them.

1.

2.

3.

Children write asking sentences (questions).
For Extra Practice, see p. 121.

6 | Writing Question Marks

An **asking sentence** begins with a **capital letter**.
An **asking sentence** ends with a **question mark**.

Is your mother here?

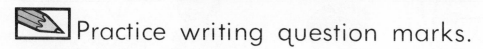 Practice writing question marks.

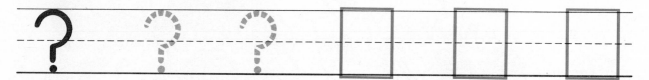

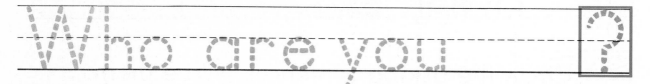 Write the correct sentence below.

1. Who are you?   who are you

Who are you ?

2. what is your name   What is your name?

_____

3. can we be friends   Can we be friends?

_____

Children write question marks and asking sentences.
For Extra Practice, see p. 122.

7 | Writing Question Words

When does he eat?

Why doesn't he fly?

Who feeds him?

Where did he come from?

What is his name?

Circle the question words in the picture. Copy them.

_____   _____

_____   _____

_____   _____

Children write question words.
For Extra Practice, see p. 123.

8 | Telling Sentences and Asking Sentences

Telling sentences end with **periods.**
Asking sentences end with **question marks.**

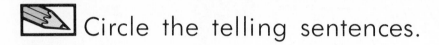 Circle the telling sentences.

1. Do you have any books?

2. (I have ten books.)

3. I like books very much.

4. My mother reads books too.

5. Do you like to read?

 Draw a line under the asking sentences.

1. When is the party?

2. I don't know.

3. How old is Patty?

4. Where does she live?

5. What will you give her?

Children identify telling sentences and asking sentences.
For Extra Practice, see p. 124.

9 | Using **I** and <u>me</u> in Sentences

My Shadow

by ROBERT LOUIS STEVENSON

I have a little shadow
that goes in and out with me,
And what can be the use of him
is more than I can see.
He is very, very like me
from the heels up to the head;
And I see him jump before me,
when I jump into my bed.

 Write **I** or **me.** Use the poem to help you.

1. _____ have a little shadow.

2. He is very, very like _____ .

3. _____ see him jump before _____ .

Children write **I** or **me** in sentences.
For Extra Practice, see p. 125.

Unit 8: More About Sentences

Building Vocabulary

Write the sound-alikes in each sentence.

bee   B

1. The _____ buzzes.

2. C comes after _____.

son   sun

3. Jay is his _____.

4. The _____ is hot.

ate   eight

5. Manuel _____ lunch.

6. Jo has _____ cats.

Children supply correct sound-alikes (homophones) in sentences.

Grammar-Writing Connection
Writing Telling and Asking Sentences

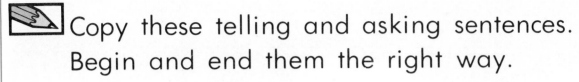Copy these telling and asking sentences. Begin and end them the right way.

1. how old are you

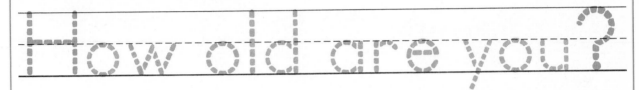

2. i am six

3. when is your birthday

4. my birthday is May 7

Children write telling and asking sentences.

Unit 8: More About Sentences

Write a telling sentence about the picture.

_____

- -

_____

- -

_____

Write an asking sentence about the picture.

_____

- -

_____

- -

_____

Children write telling and asking sentences.

Check-up: Unit 8

 Circle the two sentences.

1. milk likes cat the

2. A deer eats grass.

3. The bear runs.

4. a bee hive in sleeps

 Begin each sentence with a capital letter.

a

1. _____ dog has a tail.

tommy

2. _____ plays ball.

this

3. _____ car is blue.

 Circle the telling sentences.

1. Who are you?

2. My name is Jane.

3. Where do you go to school?

4. I am in your class.

Children review skills covered in Unit 8.

✏️ Write the asking sentences.

1. I have a pet turtle. **3.** My turtle lives in a tank.

2. Where does it live? **4.** Can it get out?

1. _____

2. _____

✏️ End these sentences the right way.

1. Where is your book ____

2. It is at home ____

3. Who wrote your book ____

4. H. A. Rey wrote this book ____

✏️ Write **me** in these sentences.

1. Sal gave _____ a kite.

2. Please play with _____.

Children review skills covered in Unit 8.

Extra Practice: Unit 8

1 | Sentences Make Sense

a raft Jack uses   (Jack uses a raft.)

 Circle the sentences.

● ▲

1. can swim I
   I can swim.

2. ducks weeds the eat
   The ducks eat weeds.

3. swim dive fish and
   Fish swim and dive.

4. a Mom boat rows
   Mom rows a boat.

 Look at the picture again.

■   Write a sentence.

Children identify sentences and write a sentence.   ● ▲ ■   **Three levels of practice**

2 | Sentences Tell

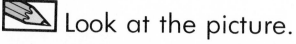 Draw a line under the telling sentences.

1. A man   A man gets on the bus.

2. The girl rides her bike.   rides her bike

3. that store   That store sells papers.

4. The light is red.   the light

5. I like the flowers.   flowers

Look at the picture.
Write your own telling sentence.

Children underline telling sentences and write a sentence.

3 | Writing Capital Letters

Begin each sentence with a word in the box. Use a capital letter.

● ▲

1. pigs   Pigs _____ eat.

2. bears   [   ] _____ sleep.

3. dogs   [   ] _____ bark.

4. Annie   [   ] _____ plays.

Look at the picture.
Write a sentence.

■

[   ] _____ .

Children capitalize the first words of sentences and write a sentence.

● ▲ ■   **Three levels of practice**   **119**

4 | Writing Periods

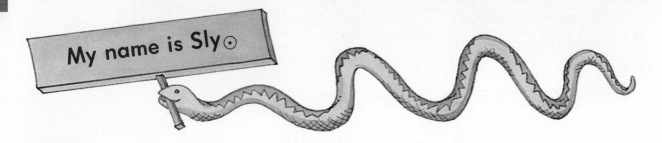

My name is Sly⊙

✏️ Put a period in the ○ at the end of
each sentence.

● ▲

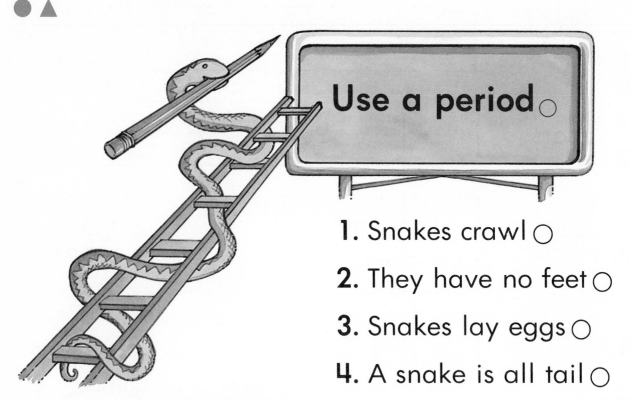

Use a period○

1. Snakes crawl○

2. They have no feet○

3. Snakes lay eggs○

4. A snake is all tail○

✏️ Write a sentence about a snake.

Children supply periods to end sentences and write
a sentence.

5 | Sentences Ask

✏️ Write each asking sentence in the picture.
● ▲

1. [ ] _____ ?

2. [ ] _____ ?

3. [ ] _____ ?

✏️ Now write an asking sentence of your own.
■

[ ] _____ ?

Children write asking sentences (questions).   ● ▲ ■   **Three levels of practice**

6 Writing Question Marks

Write a question mark
at the end of each asking sentence.

● ▲

1. What do you want to do

2. Will you go to the zoo _____

Write the correct asking
sentence on the line.

1. Can you see the bears?   can you see the bears

2. What do the bears see?   what do the bears see

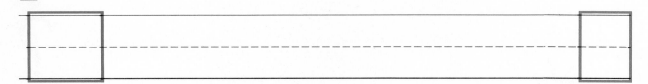

Write your own asking sentence.

Children write question marks and asking
sentences.

Name _____

7 | Writing Question Words

What is his name?

When was he born?

Who named him?

Where does he sleep?

Why is he shy?

Circle the question words in the picture. Copy them.

● ▲

1. *Why*

2. _____

3. _____

4. _____

5. _____

Write an asking sentence about the picture. Use a question word.

■

_____

_____

Children write question words and a sentence. ● ▲ ■ **Three levels of practice** **123**

8 | Telling Sentences and Asking Sentences

 Draw a line under the asking sentences.
Circle the telling sentences.

● ▲

1. Is it real?

2. (It wants to be friends.)

3. Where did it come from?

4. What is it?

5. It talked to me.

6. What did it say?

7. It likes it here.

8. It wants to stay.

 Write an asking sentence about the picture.

_____

- - - - - - - - - - - - - - - - - - -

_____

Children identify telling sentences and asking sentences and write a sentence.

9 | Using <u>I</u> and <u>me</u> in Sentences

I saw a bird.
The bird saw **me**.
I fed the bird, and
The bird sang to **me**.

✏️ Write **I** or **me** in each sentence.
Use the poem to help you.
● ▲

1. _____ looked at the monkey.

2. The monkey looked at _____.

3. _____ like the monkey.

✏️ Write a sentence. Use **I** or **me**.
■

_____

_____

Children write **I** or **me** in sentences and write a
sentence.

● ▲ ■   **Three levels of practice**   **125**

Literature and Writing
Letters

The Pickety Fence

By David McCord

The pickety fence
The pickety fence
Give it a lick it's
The pickety fence
Give it a lick it's
A clickety fence
Give it a lick it's
A lickety fence
Give it a lick
Give it a lick
Give it a lick
With a rickety stick
Pickety
Pickety
Pickety
Pick

The Letter
By Arnold Lobel

Dear Toad,
 I am glad that you are my best friend.
 Your best friend,
 Frog

COMPOSITION SKILL: LETTERS

1 | Kinds of Letters

Look at these letters. What do they tell?

Dear Carol,
    We are having fun.
I like the lake.
        Your friend,
        Alice

Dear Ling,
Please come to my
birthday party.
Day: Sunday, August 7
Time: 2:00
Place: 10 Forest Street
        Your friend,
        Abigail

Dear Auntie,
Thank you for
my book. I can
read it.
        Love,
        Daniel

Children discuss three types of letters.

COMPOSITION SKILL: LETTERS

2 ‖ Invitations

Look at this invitation.

Dear Brian,
Please come to my
birthday party.
Day: Saturday, January 8
Time: 1:00
Place: 382 Reed Road
Your friend,
Laura

Answer these questions.

1. Who will get it? _____

2. What day is the party? _____

3. What time? _____

4. Where? _____

Children discuss an invitation and write the
answers to questions about it.

COMPOSITION SKILL: LETTERS

3 | Writing an Invitation

 Fill in this invitation.

_____

Dear _____ ,

Please come to

_____

_____ •

Day: _____

Time: _____

Place: _____

_____

THE WRITING PROCESS: PREWRITING

4 | I Can Write to . . .

Who would like a letter from you?
Draw pictures of two people.

Children draw pictures of people to whom they can write and choose one.

THE WRITING PROCESS: PREWRITING

5 | I Can Tell About . . .

 What can you tell about in your letter?
Draw two pictures.

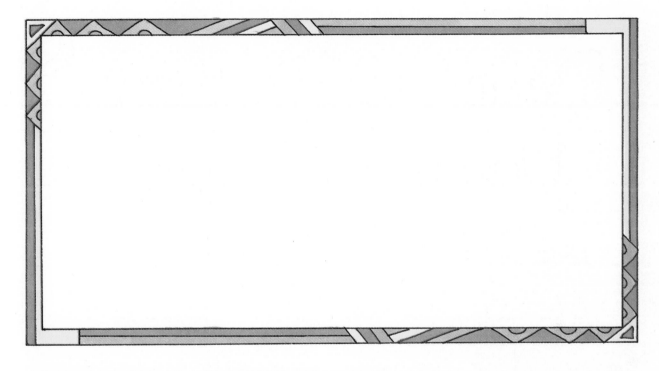

Children draw pictures of possible letter topics and choose one.

Unit 9: Letters **133**

THE WRITING PROCESS: DRAFTING

6 Pete's Letter

Pete wrote to his grandmother. Here is his first draft.

Dear Grandmother,

How are you. i like kamp. We swim We play.

Love,

Pete

Talk about Pete's letter.

Children discuss sample student letter.

THE WRITING PROCESS: DRAFTING

7 | Writing My Letter

Look at the pictures you drew in Lessons 4 and 5. Now write your letter.

Dear _____,

_____,

Children write a first draft of a letter.

Unit 9: Letters **135**

THE WRITING PROCESS: REVISING

8 | Writing More

Pete read his letter to a friend.
Then he wrote more.

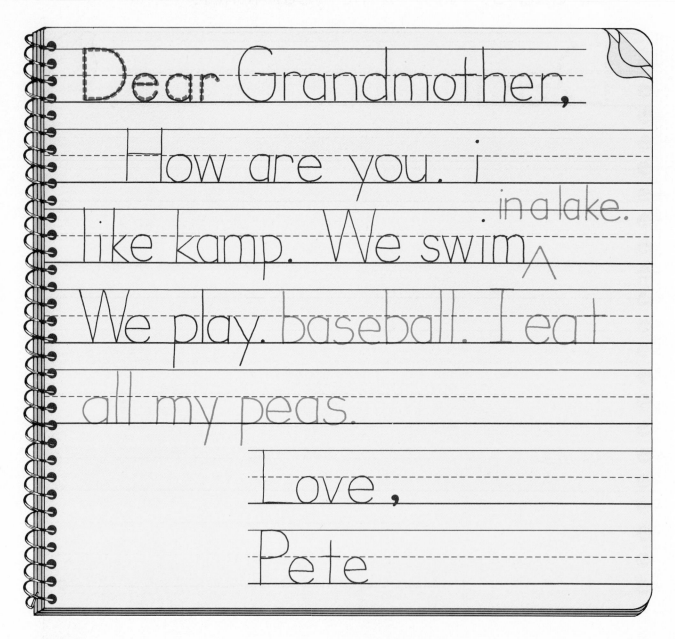

Dear Grandmother,

How are you. i
like kamp. We swim . in a lake.
We play. baseball. I eat
all my peas.

Love,

Pete

Read your letter to someone.
Talk about it. What can you add?

Children discuss the revised student sample and
revise their own letters.

9. Proofreading

Pete looked at his letter again.
He made these changes.

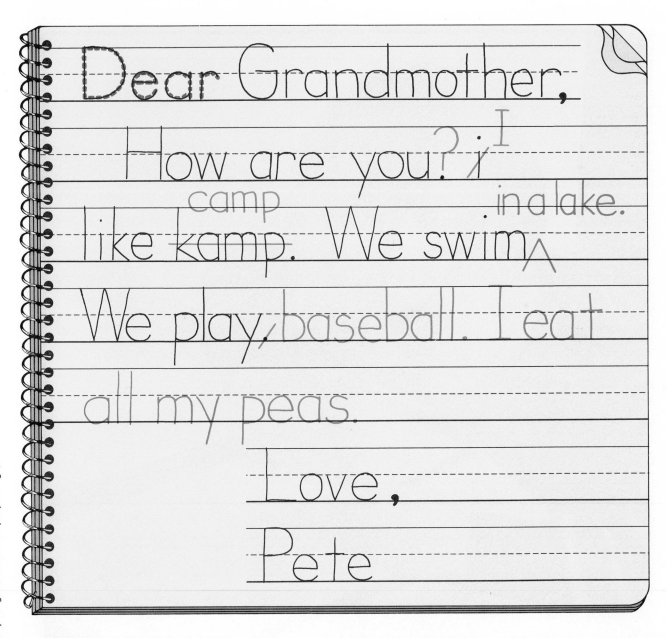

Dear Grandmother,

How are you? ~~?~~ I

like ~~kamp~~ camp. We swim ∧ in a lake.

We play baseball. I eat

all my peas.

    Love,

    Pete

 Now check your letter.
What can you change?

Children discuss the proofread student sample and
proofread their own letters.

THE WRITING PROCESS: PUBLISHING

10 Making a Final Copy

Pete wanted his letter to look neat.
He copied his letter onto another piece of paper.

 Copy your letter onto the next page.

Children make final copies of their letters.

Dear ,

,

THE WRITING PROCESS: PUBLISHING

11 | Mailing My Letter

Pete wanted to mail his letter.
Talk about what he did.

Pete Ward
25 Elm St.
Boston, MA 02108

A Nation of
Readers

Mrs. Ellen Beach
16 Overlook Road
Dallas, TX 75234

Children discuss mailing their letters.

Language and Usage
Naming Words

Name _____

1 | Naming Words

Some words are **naming words**.

boy	hat	park
dog	frog	book

✏️ Write the naming words for these pictures.

1. d o g

4. _____

2. _____

5. _____

3. _____

6. _____

Children write naming words (nouns).
For Extra Practice, see p. 160.

2 | Naming Words for People

Some **naming words** name **people**.

 Write the naming word for each person.

1.  friend

2.  man

3. 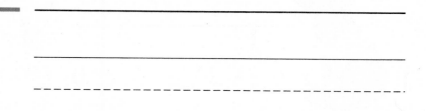 baby

4.  clown

5. 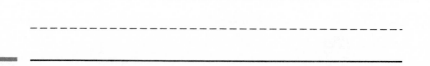 sister

6. teacher

144   **Unit 10: Naming Words**

Children write naming words (nouns) for people.
For Extra Practice, see p. 161.

3 | Naming Words for Animals

Some **naming words** name **animals**.

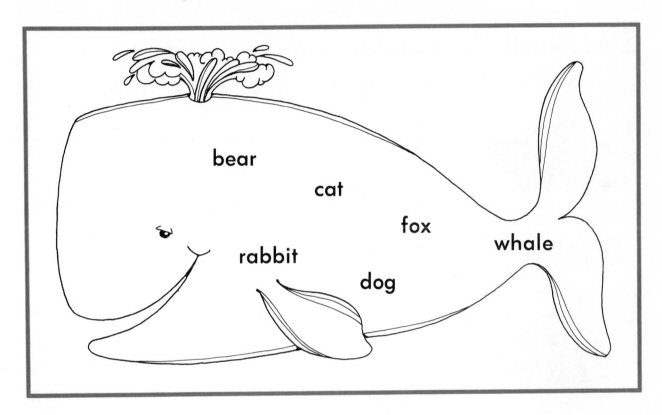

bear

cat

fox

rabbit

whale

dog

Copy the naming words for animals.

1. bear

2.

3.

4.

5.

6.

Children write naming words (nouns) for animals.
For Extra Practice, see p. 162.

Unit 10: Naming Words

4 | Naming Words for Things

Some **naming words** name **things.**

Match the pictures and the words.
Write the naming word for each thing.

1. _____

2. _____

    pencil   p̶e̶n̶c̶i̶l̶

    car

3. _____

    coat

4. _____

    boat

5. _____

    kite

6. _____

    box

Children write naming words (nouns) for things.
For Extra Practice, see p. 163.

5 | Naming Words for Places

Some **naming words** name **places**.

 Write the naming word for each place.

1.

house house

2.

pond

3.

store

4.

school

5.

park

Children write naming words (nouns) for places.
For Extra Practice, see p. 164.

6 | Naming Words in Sentences

Naming words name **people, animals, things,** and **places.**

 Finish the sentences. Use naming words from the word box.

children

street

cat

1. My pet _____cat_____ is black.

2. The _____ like school.

3. I like the houses on my _____ .

 Write a naming word for each sentence.

1. The _____ is red.

2. I saw the school _____ .

Children write naming words (nouns) in sentences.
For Extra Practice, see p. 165.

7 | One and More Than One

Some naming words mean one.

boat

Some naming words mean more than one.

boats

An **s** means more than one.

 Draw a picture for each word below.

books	trees	flowers
1.	**3.**	**5.**
ball	keys	pen
2.	**4.**	**6.**

Children distinguish between one (singular) and more than one (plural).

Unit 10: Naming Words

One and More Than One continued

hat		hats	

✏️ Circle the words that mean more than one.
Then write them.

1. father **(fathers)** _fathers_

2. homes   home

3. rooms   room

4. wing   wings

5. roads   road

✏️ Write the words. An **s** means more than one.

1. _keys_

2. _____

3. _____

150 **Unit 10: Naming Words**

Children distinguish between one (singular) and
more than one (plural).
For Extra Practice, see p. 166.

8 | Special Names

People have **special names**. **C**arol **B**en

Places have **special names**. **F**reed **P**ark

Some **animals** have **special names**. **R**uff

A **special name** begins with a **capital letter**.

 Write the special name the right way.

1. ron   Ron

3. Ann   ann

2. fluffy   Fluffy

4. denver   Denver

A **special name** begins with a **capital letter.**

Jan

Reed **S**chool

Laddie

 Circle the special names.

(Sue)	New Park	Andy
boy	Ruff	dog
Juan	Ashton	Mr. Smith
cat	Clear Lake	Liz

Write some special names.

1. your name _____

2. a friend _____

3. another friend _____

Children identify and write special names (proper nouns).
For Extra Practice, see p. 167.

9 | Days of the Week

The name of each day begins with a **capital letter**.

 Write the name of each day.

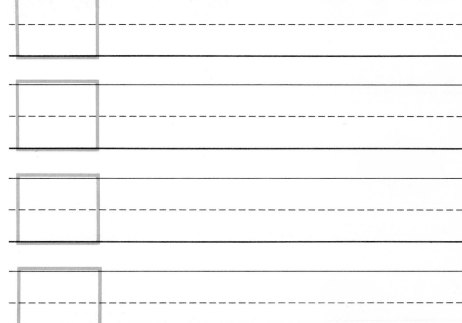

1. Sunday

2. Monday

3. Tuesday

4. Wednesday

5. Thursday

6. Friday

7. Saturday

Children write and capitalize the days of the week.
For Extra Practice, see p. 168.

10 | Months of the Year

The name of each month begins with
a **capital letter**.

January 	February	March	April
May	June	July	August
September	October	November	December

✏️ Write the month for each special day.

1.

Halloween ___October___

2.

Valentine's Day ___[ ]___

3.

Thanksgiving ___[ ]___

Children write and capitalize months of the year.
For Extra Practice, see p. 169.

11 | Seasons of the Year

The seasons are **fall**, **winter**, **spring**, and **summer**.
The names of the seasons <u>do not</u> begin with capital letters.

September
October
November

December
January
February

March
April
May

June
July
August

 Finish these sentences.

1. Thanksgiving is in the 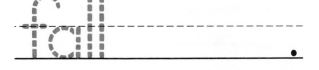.

2. My favorite season is .

3. My birthday is in the _____.

Children write the seasons of the year.
For Extra Practice, see p. 170.

USAGE

12 | <u>h</u>e, <u>s</u>he, <u>i</u>t

He, **she**, and **it** can take the place of naming words.

Draw a line to **he**, **she**, or **it**.

1. Linda   she
                  he

2. grandfather   he
                  it

3. bed   he
                  it

4. kite   she
                  it

Write **he**, **she**, or **it**.

1. sister   she

2. brother   _____

3. hat   _____

4. ball   _____

5. girl   _____

6. teacher   _____

156   **Unit 10: Naming Words**

Children write **he**, **she**, **it** (pronouns).
For Extra Practice, see p. 171.

Building Vocabulary

Some words are made from two words.

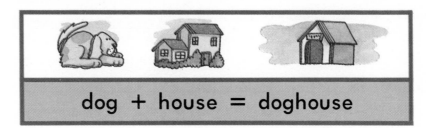

dog + house = doghouse

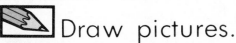 Add two words to make a new word.
Write the new words.

1. door + bell = doorbell

2. foot + ball = _____

3. star + fish = _____

Draw pictures.

birdhouse	sidewalk

Children write compound words.

Grammar-Writing Connection
Writing Naming Words in Sentences

Finish these sentences with special names.

1. My name is _____ •

2. I go to _____ School.

3. This month is _____ •

4. Monday comes after _____ •

Write a sentence about this picture.

Children complete sentences with naming words
(nouns) and write an original sentence.

Check-up: Unit 10

 Write the naming words for these pictures.

1. _____

2. _____

3. _____

4. _____

 Write the words for the pictures.

1. _____

2. _____

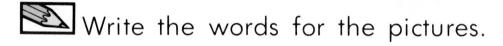 Draw a line under the special names.

boy Jack	cat Fluffy	road East Road
1.	2.	3.

Draw a line under the right word.

january January	Wednesday wednesday	June june	monday Monday	Spring spring
1.	2.	3.	4.	5.

Children review skills covered in Unit 10.

Extra Practice: Unit 10

1 Naming Words

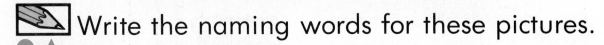

eggs   girl   farm   hen

 Write the naming words for these pictures.

1. farm

3. _____

2. _____

4. _____

Write a sentence. Use a naming word.

_____

- - - - - - - - - - - - - - - - - - - -

_____

Children write naming words (nouns) and a sentence.

2 | Naming Words for People

 Write the naming word for each **person**.

1.  girl

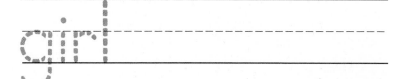

2.  boy

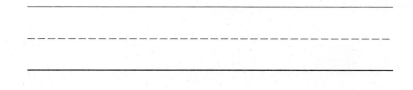

3.  father

4.  mother

5.  helper

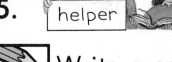 Write a sentence.
   Use a word that names a person.

Children write naming words (nouns) for people
and write a sentence.

● ▲ ■   **Three levels of practice**   **161**

3 | Naming Words for Animals

deer

bee

mouse

rabbit

✏ Copy the naming words for **animals**.
● ▲

1. deer

3.

2.

4.

✏ Write a sentence.
Use a word that names an animal.

_____

_____

Children write naming words (nouns) for animals and write a sentence.

4 | Naming Words for Things

 Match the pictures and the words.
Write the naming word for each **thing**.

● ▲

1.

2.

3.

4.

pool _____

fan   ̲f̲a̲n̲

apple _____

sun _____

 Write a sentence.
Use a word that names
a thing.

■

I ♥ naming words

_____

_____

Children write naming words (nouns) for things and
write a sentence.

● ▲ ■   **Three levels of practice**   **163**

5 | Naming Words for Places

Write the naming word for each **place**.
● ▲

sea   **1.** sea

road   **2.** _____

woods   **3.** _____

house   **4.** _____

Write a sentence.
Use a word that names a place.

_____

_____

_____

Children write naming words (nouns) for places and write a sentence.

6 | Naming Words in Sentences

 Finish the sentences.
Use naming words from the word box.

●▲

city   dog   mom

1. My _mom_ _____ works hard.

2. She walks the _____ .

3. She drives to the _____ .

 Look at the picture.
Write a sentence.

■

_____

_____

_____

Children write naming words (nouns) in sentences
and write a sentence.

●▲■ **Three levels of practice** **165**

7 | One and More Than One

frog

frogs

 Circle the words that mean more than one.
Then write them.

● ▲

1. ant   (ants)

2. caps   cap

3. hills   hill

4. shoe   shoes

 Write a sentence. Use a word
that means more than one.

Children distinguish between one and more than
one and write a sentence.

8 | Special Names

 Write the special name the right way.

1. abby   Abby

Abby

3. Bozo   bozo

2. Tot Park   tot park

4. jack   Jack

 Draw a friend.
Write a sentence with
the name of your friend.

Children write special names (proper nouns) and
write a sentence.

● ▲ ■   **Three levels of practice**   167

9 | Days of the Week

Sunday   Monday   Tuesday   Wednesday   Thursday   Friday   Saturday

 Finish the sentences.
Use names for different days.

1. On Monday   I cook.

2. On ☐   I look.

3. Each ☐   I go.

4. On ☐   I sew.

 Write a sentence.
Use the name of a day.

_____

- - - - - - - - - - - - - - - - -

_____

Children write and capitalize the days of the week
and write a sentence.

10 | Months of the Year

January 	February	March	April
May	June	July	August
September	October	November	December

✏️ Finish each sentence
with the name of a month.

● ▲

1. It can rain a lot in _April_ .

2. I go back to school in ☐ .

3. August follows ☐ .

✏️ Write a sentence.
■ Use the name of a month.

_____

- - - - - - - - - - - - - - - - -

_____

Children write and capitalize months of the year
and write a sentence.

 Three levels of practice   169

11 | Seasons of the Year

fall

September
October
November

winter

December
January
February

spring

March
April
May

summer

June
July
August

 Write the name of the right season.
● ▲

1. It rains a lot in  spring   .

2. I love the hot days of _____ .

3. In the _____ school starts.

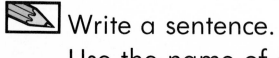 Write a sentence.
   Use the name of a season.

_____

_____

_____

Children write the seasons of the year and write a sentence.

12 | he, she, it

Write **he, she,** or **it**.
● ▲

1. teacher *she*

4. dad _____

2. desk _____

5. moon _____

3. man _____

6. Jill _____

Write a sentence about the picture. Use **he, she,** or **it**.

■

_____

- - - - - - - - - - - - - - - -

_____

Children write he, she, or it (pronouns) and write a sentence.

● ▲ ■   **Three levels of practice**   **171**

Literature and Writing
Story

Move Over

By Lilian Moore

Big
burly
bumblebee
buzzing
through the grass,
move over.

Black and
yellow
clover rover,
let me pass.

Fat and
furry
rumblebee
loud on the
wing,
let me
hurry
past
your sting.

173

The Owl

By Jack Prelutsky

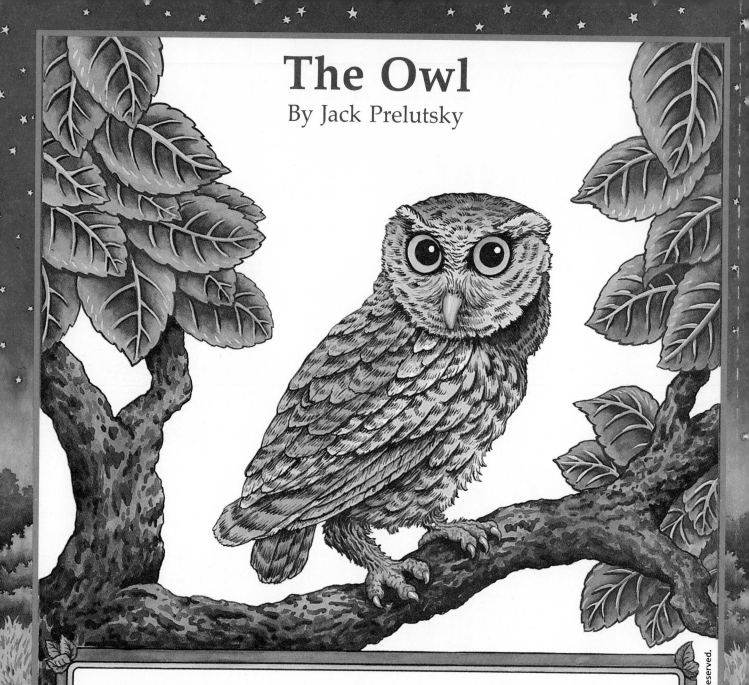

The owl is wary, the owl is wise.
He knows all the names of the stars
in the skies.
He hoots and he toots and he lives
by his wits,
but mostly he sits . . . and he sits . . . and
he sits.

The Lion and the Mouse

from Aesop retold by Marie Gaudette

One day, Lion came down from a tree. It had been a long hot day. Lion was hungry. But he was too tired to hunt for his supper.

"I will rest now," said Lion. "When it is dark, I will hunt."

Lion lay down in the tall yellow grass. He went to sleep.

Lion had pale yellow hair. It looked just like the grass. It fooled a little mouse. The mouse ran right up on Lion's back.

Listen to the rest of the story.

COMPOSITION SKILL: STORY

1 | Beginning, Middle, End

 Talk about the pictures.

 Draw what happens.

Children discuss the beginning and the middle of a story and
provide an ending for it.

Unit 11: Story   177

Name _____

2 | Story Ideas

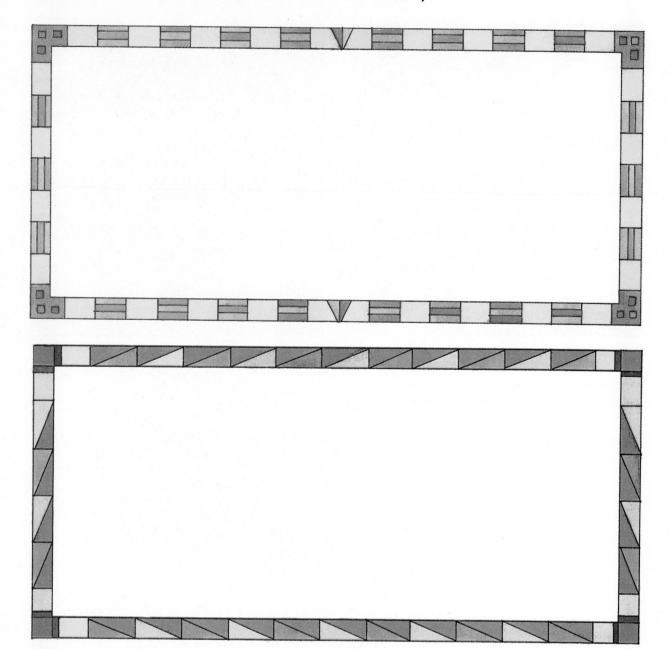

Draw two ideas for a story.

Talk about your pictures with someone.
Choose one for a story.

Children draw pictures of possible story topics and choose one.

THE WRITING PROCESS: PREWRITING

3 | Getting Ready to Write

 Draw what will happen at the beginning of your story.

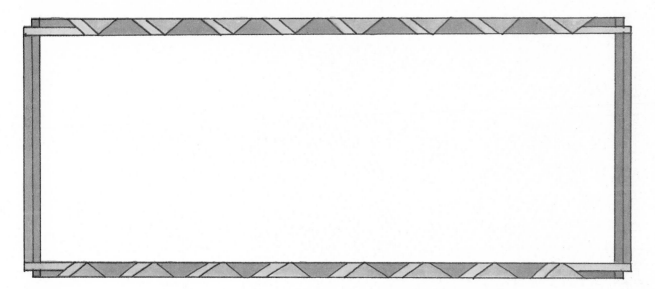

Draw what will happen at the end.

Now tell your story to someone.

THE WRITING PROCESS: DRAFTING

4 | Jan's Story

Jan wrote a story. Here is her first draft.

I found a box? Joe found a ball. There ws a magic key. i opened the box.

 Talk about Jan's story.

Children discuss the first draft of a sample story.

THE WRITING PROCESS: DRAFTING

5 | Writing My Story

 Look back at the pictures you drew in Lesson 3. Write your story.

Children write a first draft of the story they told in Lesson 3.

THE WRITING PROCESS: REVISING

6 | Writing More

Jan read her story to Kevin.
Then she made changes.

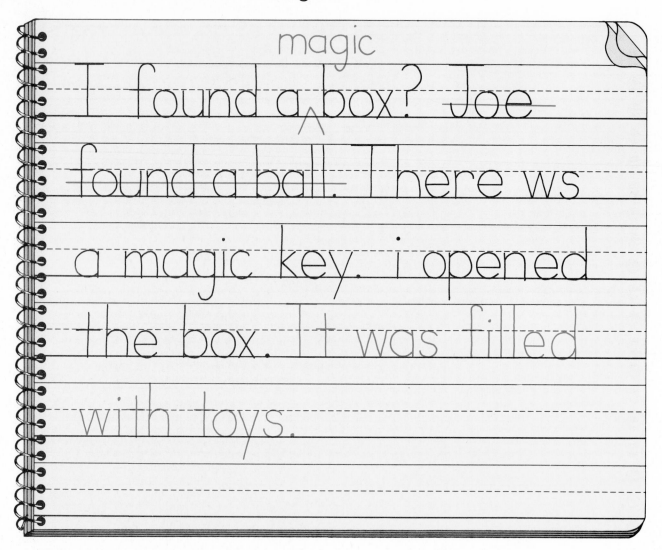

magic

I found a box? ~~Joe~~
~~found a ball.~~ There ws
a magic key. i opened
the box. It was filled
with toys.

Read your story to someone.
Talk about it.
What can you add?
What can you change?

Children discuss the revised student sample and revise their own stories.

THE WRITING PROCESS: PROOFREADING

7 | Proofreading

Jan looked at her story one more time.
She made these changes.

Now check your story.
What can you change?

Children discuss the proofread student sample and
proofread their own stories.

THE WRITING PROCESS: PUBLISHING

8 | Making a Final Copy

Jan wanted her story to look neat.
She copied her story onto another piece
of paper. She wrote a title.

Think of a title for your story.
Write your story on the next page.

Children add a title and copy their final drafts.

9 | Making My Book

Jan made her story into a book.

Make your story into a book.
Use the covers in the back of this book.

Children make books of their finished stories and
share them in class.

1 | Action Words

Some **action words** tell
what people and
animals do.

The boys **sing**.

 Draw a line under each action word.

1. The boys run.

4. The men talk.

2. The boys hop.

5. The children laugh.

3. The girls read.

6. The girls jump.

Children underline action words (verbs).

Unit 12: Action Words 189

Some **action words** tell
what people and
animals do.

The ducks **walk.**

Match the pictures and the words.
Write each action word.

1. _____

2. _____

3. _____

4. _____

5. _____

6. _____

play

eat

jump

fly

run

sing

play ⌜play⌝ _____

_____

_____

_____

_____

_____

Children write action words (verbs).
For Extra Practice, see p. 207.

Name _____

2 | Action Words with One and More

Some action words tell about more than one.

The bells ring.

Some girls jump.

Some action words tell about one.
Action words that tell about one end in **s**.

The bell ring**s**.

A girl jump**s**.

 Write the action word for each picture.

1. This dog .

runs

2. The boys _____.

talk

3. My little sister _____.

sits

Children write action words (verbs) that agree in
number with subjects of sentences.

Action Words with One and More continued

This cat sits.   Three cats sit.

 Write the correct action word.

1. A dog ~barks~ •
   barks
   bark

2. The dogs _____ •
   barks
   bark

3. The boy _____ •
   sings
   sing

4. Six boys _____ •
   sings
   sing

Children write action words (verbs) that agree in
number with subjects of sentences.
For Extra Practice, see p. 208.

USAGE

3 | is and are

Use **is** in a sentence about one.
Use **are** in a sentence about more than one.

This boy **is** happy.

These boys **are** happy.

Circle **is** or **are** to finish each sentence.

1. This girl (is are) six.

2. The bird (is are) small.

3. These girls (is are) friends.

4. Many birds (is are) here.

5. This duck (is are) big.

Children circle **is** and **are** in sentences.

<u>is</u> and <u>are</u> continued

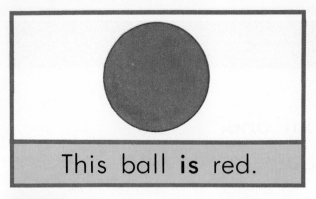 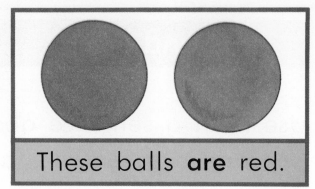

| This ball **is** red. | These balls **are** red. |

 Write **is** or **are** to finish each sentence.

1. The tables _____ long.
    is   are

2. His car _____ green.
    is   are

3. This box _____ big.
    is   are

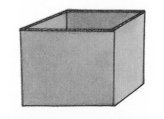

4. Some cats _____ brown.
    is   are

5. This baby _____ happy.
    is   are

194   **Unit 12: Action Words**

Children write **is** and **are** in sentences.
For Extra Practice, see p. 209.

4 | Adding ed

Add **ed** to some action words to tell about the past.

Now	Past
I play now.	I play**ed** last night.
I jump today.	I jump**ed** yesterday.

 Add **ed** to each action word.

1. We ___painted___ after lunch.

2. We ___rest___ yesterday.

3. Last week I ___call___ Grandfather.

4. Yesterday Grandmother ___call___ .

5. Last night we ___walk___ home.

Children add **ed** to action words (verbs) in the present and past tenses.

Unit 12: Action Words   **195**

Adding ed continued

Add **ed** to some action words to tell what happened in the past.

 Draw a line under the action words that tell about the past.

1. quacked

2. ask

3. talked

4. showed

5. play

6. laughed

7. work

8. walked

9. looked

10. walk

11. rolled

12. played

 Write these words in the sentences.

counted	jumped	cooked

1. The cat _____ into the boat.

2. We _____ the money.

3. Dad _____ breakfast.

Children choose and write action words (verbs) in the past tense.
For Extra Practice, see p. 210.

5 | Action Words in Sentences

Some action words tell what people and animals do.

 Complete each sentence with an action word from the box.

works	swims	eat	sleeps	help

1. My dog sleeps in a bed.

2. The men _____ lunch.

3. I _____ my father.

4. A bear _____ in the lake.

5. Mr. Long _____ at the school.

Children complete sentences with action words (verbs).

Action Words in Sentences continued

Look at the pictures.
Write an action word for each sentence.

1. The little rabbit _____ •

2. Sue and Bill _____ wood.

3. Mrs. James _____ the cars.

Children complete sentences with action
words (verbs).
For Extra Practice, see p. 211.

USAGE

6 | <u>was</u> and <u>were</u>

Use **was** in a sentence about one.
Use **were** in a sentence about more than one.

This dog **was** in.

These dogs **were** out.

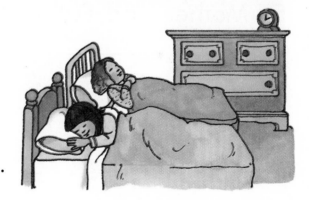

Write **was** or **were**.

1. Jan ＿＿＿＿＿ sick.
   was   were

2. Ann and Rosa ＿＿＿＿＿ asleep.
   was   were

3. Father ＿＿＿＿＿ at home.
   was   were

Children write **was** and **were** in sentences.

Unit 12: Action Words

was and were continued

Bob was hot.

Jill and Jim were cold.

 Draw a line under the correct word.

1. The girls (was <u>were</u>) lost.

2. Sue (was were) sad.

3. Juanita (was were) scared.

4. Soon the girls (was were) back.

5. Mother and Father (was were) happy.

 Write **was** or **were**.

1. Two ducks _____ here.

2. One cup _____ on the table.

Children write **was** and **were** correctly in sentences.
For Extra Practice, see p. 212.

7 | isn't, don't, can't

Isn't means **is not.**
Don't means **do not.**
Can't means **cannot.**

This mark **,** takes the place of missing letters.

Match the words that mean the same.

is not ——————————— don't

cannot ————————— isn't

do not   can't

Write each word.

1. _____

2. _____

3. _____

Children match and write **isn't, don't,** and **can't** (contractions).

<u>isn't</u>, <u>don't</u>, <u>can't</u> continued

Write **isn't, don't,** or **can't.**

1. Mary _____ my sister.

2. They _____ live there.

3. Bud _____ swim.

Write **don't, isn't,** or **can't.**

1. I do not see Bob.

   I _____ see Bob.

2. He is not here.

   He _____ here.

3. We cannot find him.

   We _____ find him.

Children write **isn't, don't,** and **can't** (contractions) in sentences.
For Extra Practice, see p. 213.

Building Vocabulary

 Write the better action word.

1. He ___marched___ in the parade.

marched   walked

2. Ted _____ under the table.

goes   crawls

3. Paula _____ the milk.

pours   spills

4. The kitten _____ up.

jumps   gets

Children choose and write the more precise action
word (verb) in each sentence.

Grammar-Writing Connection
Writing Action Words in Sentences

Look at the picture. Write two sentences about what the people are doing.

1.

2.

Children write sentences.

Name _____

Check-up: Unit 12

 Write the correct action word.

_____

------------------------------------ sing

1. The girl _____ • sings

_____

------------------------------------ eat

2. Three cats _____ • eats

_____

------------------ is

3. Matt _____ tall.   are

_____

---------------------- is

4. Matt and Bob _____ tall.   are

 Draw a line under the action words that tell about the past.

1. walked   4. talked

2. jump   5. helped

3. laughed   6. call

Children review skills covered in Unit 12.

Write the correct action word.

1. We _____ now.   play
   played

2. Last week I _____ my room.   clean
   cleaned

 Draw a line under the correct word.

1. Dad (was were) home.

2. Mom and I (was were) glad.

Write the words that mean the same.

1. do not _____

2. is not _____

3. cannot _____

isn't
can't
don't

Children review skills covered in Unit 12.

Extra Practice: Unit 12

1 | Action Words

 Match the pictures and the words.

● ▲ Write each action word.

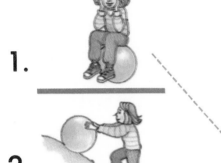 1. _____

_____ push _____

 2. _____

_____ roll _____

 3. _____

_____ sit ṡ̇i̇ṫ _____

 4. _____

_____ wave _____

 Write your own sentence.

_____

_____

Children write action words (verbs) and write a
sentence.

● ▲ ■ **Three levels of practice**   **207**

2 | Action Words with One and More

The girl run**s**.

The children run.

 Write the correct action word.

1. A boy ~~runs~~ .

run
runs

2. Paulo and Maria _____ .

run
runs

3. Ruff _____ .

race
races

4. Mom and Dad _____ .

jog
jogs

5. Some boys _____ .

jump
jumps

Write a sentence about the picture.

_____

_____

_____

Children write action words (verbs) that agree in number with subjects of sentences and write a sentence.

Name _____

3 | is and are

| This car **is** red. | These cars **are** blue. |

 Write **is** or **are** to finish each sentence.

1. This beach __is__ fun.
   is   are

2. The shells _____ pretty.
   is   are

3. Some birds _____ white.
   is   are

4. A whale _____ big.
   is   are

Write a sentence. Use **is** or **are**.

_____

Children write **is** and **are** in sentences and write a sentence.

● ▲ ■   **Three levels of practice**   **209**

Name _____

 4 | **Adding <u>ed</u>**

 Write these words in the sentences.
● ▲

barked   jumped   saved

_____

- -

1. The dog _____ at the cat.

_____

- -

2. The cat _____ up a tree.

_____

- -

3. Stephen _____ his cat.

 Write a sentence.
Use an action word that tells about the past.

_____

- -

Children choose and write action words (verbs) in the past tense and write a sentence.

Name _____

5 | Action Words in Sentences

Complete each sentence with an action word from the box.

● ▲

| clean | cuts | sleeps | work |

1. We _work_ _____ at home.

2. Mom _____ the grass.

3. Sis and I _____ our room.

4. Our cat Fang just _____ .

Write a sentence about the picture.

■

_____

_____

Children complete sentences with action words
(verbs) and write a sentence.

● ▲ ■   **Three levels of practice**

6 | <u>was</u> and <u>were</u>

The star **was** bright.   The stars **were** bright.

Draw a line under the correct word.
● ▲

1. The weather (<u>was</u> were) cool.

2. The days (was were) shorter.

3. Fall (was were) here.

4. I (was were) happy.

5. The leaves (was were) red and gold.

6. This day (was were) perfect.

Write a sentence. Use **was** or **were**.

■

_ _

_____

Children write **was** and **were** correctly in sentences and write a sentence.

7 || isn't, don't, can't

Isn't means is not

Don't means do not

Can't means cannot

 Write **isn't**, **don't**, or **can't**.
● ▲

1. This is not my letter.

_____

- - - - - - - - - - - - - - - -

This _____ my letter.

2. The Browns do not live here.

_____

- - - - - - - - - - - - - - - - -

The Browns _____ live here.

3. I cannot help you.

_____

- - - - - - - - - - - - - - - - -

I _____ help you.

 Write a sentence about the
picture. Use **isn't**, **don't**, or **can't**.
■
_____

- -

_____

Children write **isn't**, **don't**, and **can't** in sentences
and write a sentence.

● ▲ ■ **Three levels of practice** 213

Name _____

Look at the pictures.
Write the words from the boxes that
describe what you see.

flowers

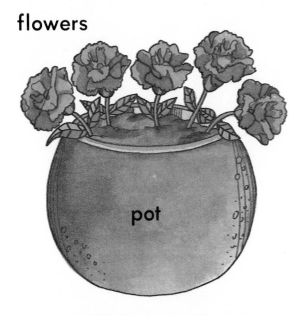

pot

flowers

pot

| big   red |
| five |

| little   blue |
| three |

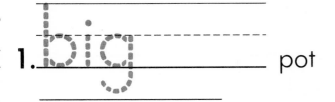

1. big _____ pot

2. _____ flowers

3. _____ flowers

4. _____ pot

5. _____ flowers

6. _____ flowers

Children write describing words (adjectives).
For Extra Practice, see p. 227.

Unit 13: Describing Words   **215**

2 | Describing Taste, Smell, and Sound

 Write the words from the box that describe taste, smell, and sound.

1. The pickle tastes .

| sweet |
| loud |
| sour |

2. This flower smells _____.

3. The drum sounds _____.

 Match the words and pictures.

1. salty

2. sour

3. soft

4. loud

Children write and match describing words (adjectives).
For Extra Practice, see p. 228.

3 | Describing How Things Feel

How would each thing feel?
Write a word from the box.

soft	cold	wet
hard	hot	dry

1.

soft

3.

_____

5.

_____

2.

_____

4.

_____

6.

_____

Children write describing words (adjectives).
For Extra Practice, see p. 229.

Unit 13: Describing Words   **217**

Name

4 | Using Describing Words

Look at the word box. Write the words that describe each picture.

wet shoe	long bat	red rug
dry shoe	short bat	blue rug

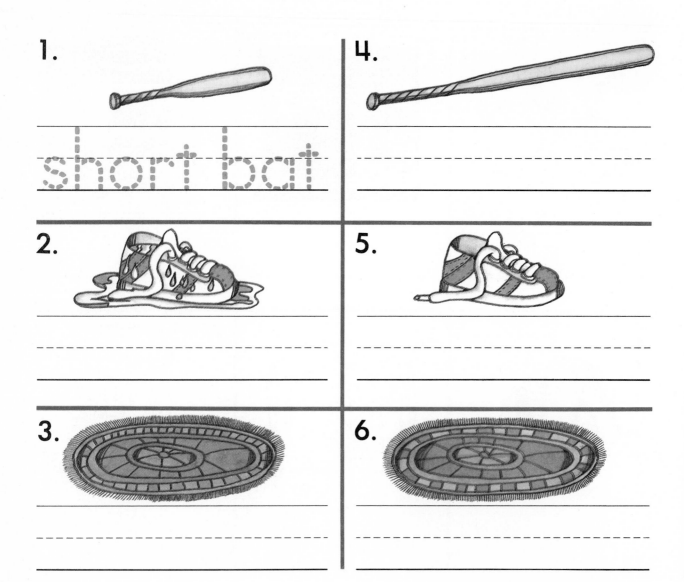

1. short bat

4.

2.

5.

3.

6.

Children write descriptions of pictures.
For Extra Practice, see p. 230.

5 | Describing Words in Sentences

Describing words tell how things look, taste, smell, sound, and feel.

 Use describing words from the box. Finish the sentences.

fresh	sweet	loud	hot	square

1. The country air smells  **fresh**.

2. A pear tastes _____ .

3. The window is _____ .

4. The toy made a _____ sound.

5. The _____ soup is here.

Children complete sentences, using describing words (adjectives).
For Extra Practice, see p. 231.

Unit 13: Describing Words 219

6 | Choosing the Better Description

✏️ Circle the words that tell more
about each picture.

1.

a toy

(a brown teddy bear)

2.

a long yellow kitchen

a room

3.

an animal

a little green frog

✏️ Write the word from each box that
describes the picture.

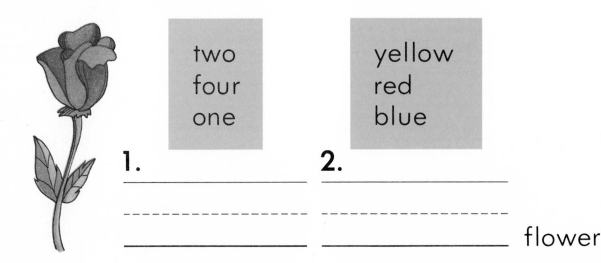

two	yellow
four	red
one	blue

1. _____

2. _____ flower

Children choose the better of two descriptions.
For Extra Practice, see p. 232.

7 | Adding er and est

Look at the brushes. How are they different?

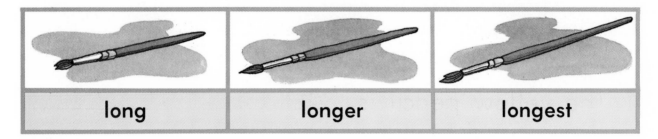

| long | longer | longest |

Add **er** and **est** to the first word.
Write the new words.

tall

1.

taller

3.

tallest

fast

2.

4.

Adding <u>er</u> and <u>est</u> continued

Finish the sentences.

| short | shorter | shortest |

1. The yellow pencil is  short.

2. The green pencil is _____ .

3. The red pencil is _____ .

| large | larger | largest |

1. The brown house is _____ .

2. The blue house is _____ .

3. The red house is _____ .

222   **Unit 13: Describing Words**

Children complete sentences with comparative and
superlative forms of adjectives.
For Extra Practice, see p. 233.

Building Vocabulary

Listen. Draw a line under the right picture.

Children listen and underline the picture that
illustrates the correct homograph.

Unit 13: Describing Words 223

Grammar-Writing Connection
Writing Describing Words in Sentences

Write two sentences that tell about the picture. Use describing words.

1. _____

_____

_____ •

2. _____

_____

_____ •

Children generate and write descriptive sentences.

Check-up: Unit 13

 Circle three words that describe
the rabbits.

red   soft   sour   one   two   brown

 Circle two words that describe ice.

soft   hard   green   cold

Draw lines to match the words and
the pictures.

1. small

2. smaller

3. smallest

Children review skills covered in Unit 13.

Circle the words that tell how things feel.

warm   green   wet   cold

Finish the sentences. Use words from the box.

blue   hot   clean   sweet

1. The stove feels _____ .

2. A grape tastes _____ .

3. Her hair smells _____ .

4. The sky looks _____ today.

Circle the words that tell more.

1. a plant | a tall green tree

2. an animal | a furry white bunny

3. this cold blue lake | water

Children review skills covered in Unit 13.

Extra Practice: Unit 13

1 | Looking and Describing

 Look at the pictures.

●▲ Describe them using the words in the box.

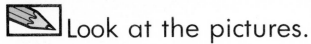

brown	sad	new
old	happy	gray

1. new _____ toy   4. _____ toy

2. _____ toy   5. _____ toy

3. _____ toy   6. _____ toy

Write a sentence about one bear.
Use a word from the box.

■

_____

_____

Name _____

2 | Describing Taste, Smell, and Sound

✏️ Match the words and pictures.
Then write the words.

● ▲

1. _____

    loud _____

2. _____

    soft _____

3. _____

    sour   sour _____

4. _____

    salty _____

5. _____

    sweet _____

✏️ Write a sentence.
Tell about taste, smell, or sound.

▮

_____

_____

_____

Children match and write describing words
(adjectives) and write a sentence.

3 | Describing How Things Feel

 How would each thing feel?
Write a word from the box.

cold	sharp	soft
hot	smooth	wet

1. wet   3. _____   5. _____

 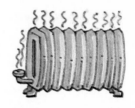

2. _____   4. _____   6. _____

 Write a sentence.
Use a word from the box.

_____

_____

Children write describing words (adjectives) and
write a sentence.

 Three levels of practice   229

4 | Using Describing Words

 Look at the word box. Write the words that describe each picture.

● ▲

happy boy	tall girl
sad boy	short girl

1. tall girl

2.

3. _____

4.

 Now write a sentence.
Use a word from the box.

old   fast

_____

Children write descriptions of pictures and write a sentence.

5 | Describing Words in Sentences

Use describing words from the box. Finish the sentences.

● ▲

| fresh   loud   red   warm |

1. Come into our __red_____ barn.

2. The hay smells _____ .

3. Our cow makes a _____ MOO!

4. She likes her _____ home.

Look at the picture.
Write a sentence.

_____

_____

Children complete sentences using describing words
(adjectives) and write a sentence.

● ▲ ■   **Three levels of practice**   **231**

6 Choosing the Better Description

 Circle the words that tell more
about each picture.

● ▲

1.

water

(a small pretty pond)

2.

a toy

a tiny sailboat

3.

a raft

a long wooden raft

4.

one big jumping fish

an animal

 Look at the picture.
Write a sentence.
Use two describing words.

_____

- - - - - - - - - - - - - - - - - - - -

_____

Children choose the better of two descriptions and
write a sentence.

7 | Adding <u>er</u> and <u>est</u>

 Add **er** and **est** to the first word.
Write the new words.

●▲

old   1. older   2. _____

slow   3. _____   4. _____

bright   5. _____   6. _____

 Write a sentence.
Use a word you wrote with **er** or **est**.

■

_____

_____

Children write comparative and superlative forms
of adjectives and write a sentence.   ●▲■ **Three levels of practice**   **233**

1 | The Library

A **library** is a place where many books are kept. You may borrow these books and take them home.

books   records/tapes   filmstrips

librarian

read

listen

look

Write a sentence about what you would see or do in a library.

Children discuss and write about the resources in a library.

2 | Thinking About a Book

 Listen to a book.
The **title** is The Forgetful Bears.
The **author** is Lawrence Weinberg.

The **Forgetful Bears**

LAWRENCE WEINBERG

Illustrated by PAULA WINTER

Tell what you liked about the book.

Children listen to a book and discuss what they
liked about it.

3 | Sharing a Book

Kim wrote a book report.
Talk about what she wrote.

Title: __The Forgetful Bears__

Author: __Lawrence Weinberg__

This book is about __bears.__

__They forget__

__everything.__

I like this book because __it is__

__very funny.__

Children discuss a sample student book report.

4 | A Book I Like

Write the title.

Draw a picture of something that happens in the book.

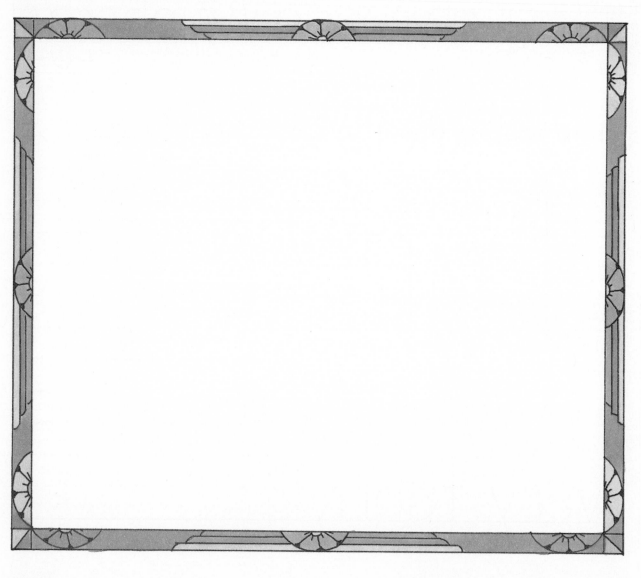

Children write titles of books they like and draw pictures of what happens in those books.

Name

5 | My Book Report

 Write about your book.

Title: _____

Author: _____

This book is about _____

I like this book because _____

Student's Handbook

Study Skills Lessons

1 Words in ABC Order

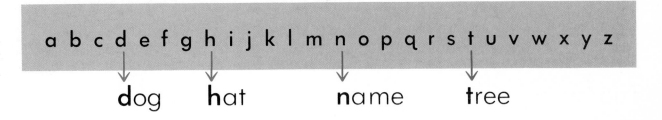

a b c d e f g h i j k l m n o p q r s t u v w x y z

dog   **h**at   **n**ame   **t**ree

The words **dog, hat, name,** and **tree** are in **ABC order.**

Look at the words in each picture frame. Circle the first letter of each word. If the three words are in ABC order, color the frame red.

apple
bike
hat

kite
egg
doll

ring
sun
tent

mop
net
rug

2 Words in a Dictionary

a b c d e f g h i j k l m n o p q r s t u v w x y z

A **dictionary** is a book about words.
The words or pictures in a dictionary
are in ABC order.

Circle the word that comes first
in a dictionary.

1.

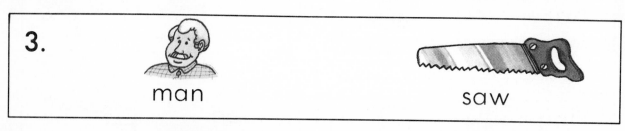

pencil   (fish)

2.

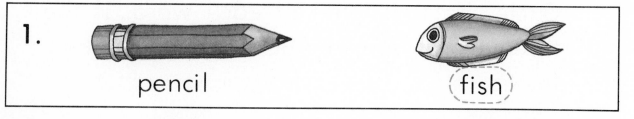

hat   coat

3.

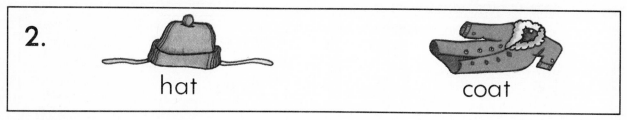

man   saw

4.

turtle   rabbit

Children decide which word appears first
in a dictionary.

3 Using a Dictionary

Words that begin with the same letter are in the same part of a dictionary. The words **children**, **coat**, and **cow** are in the **C** part.

✏️ Circle the words you would find in the **B** part of a dictionary.

(boat)   cat   bat   box

book   girl   bird   bed

✏️ In which part of a dictionary would you find each word? Write the letter.

jar _____

duck _____

key _____

boat _____

Children determine where in a dictionary they would look for certain words.

4 Using My Picture Dictionary

 Find each picture in your Picture Dictionary. Write the word for each picture.

1. _____ apple

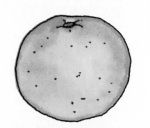

2. _____

3. _____

4. _____

5. _____

Student's Handbook: Study Skills Lessons

Children find and write words from the Picture Dictionary, pp. 246-254.

5 Finding More Words

Find each word in your Picture Dictionary. Write another word that you find under the same letter.

1. bird   boy

2. face

3. line

4. paint

5. store

Children find and write additional words from the Picture Dictionary, pp. 246-254.

Picture Dictionary

Aa	Bb	Cc
animals	bird	children
apple	book	coat
arm	boy	cow

Children use the Picture Dictionary for spelling help and for dictionary lessons. Throughout the year, they add their own words on the lines provided.

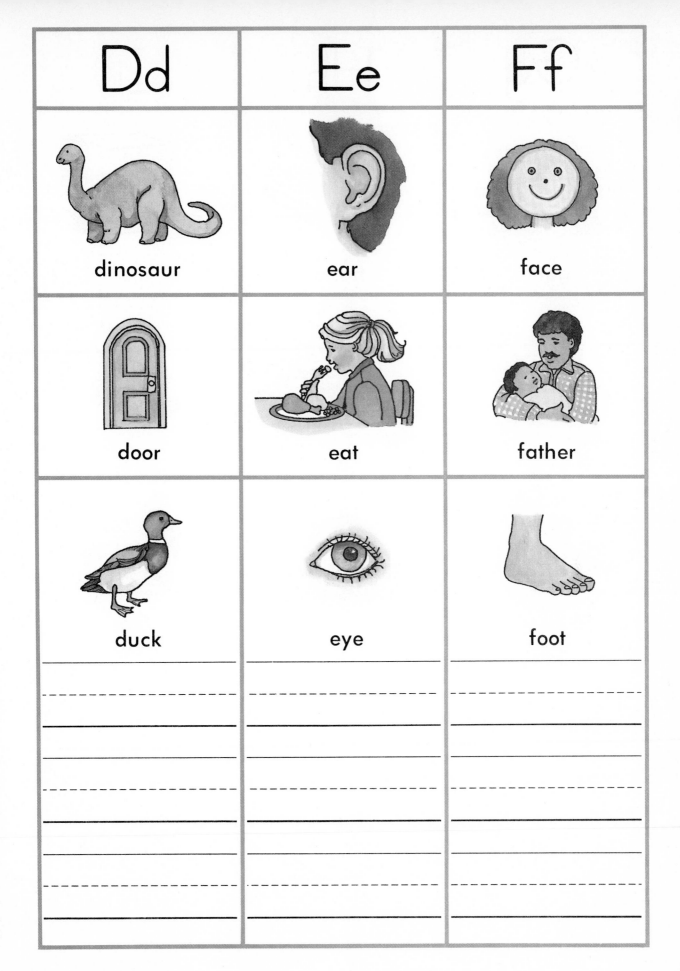

Dd	Ee	Ff
dinosaur	ear	face
door	eat	father
duck	eye	foot

Children use the Picture Dictionary for spelling help and for dictionary lessons. Throughout the year, they add their own words on the lines provided.

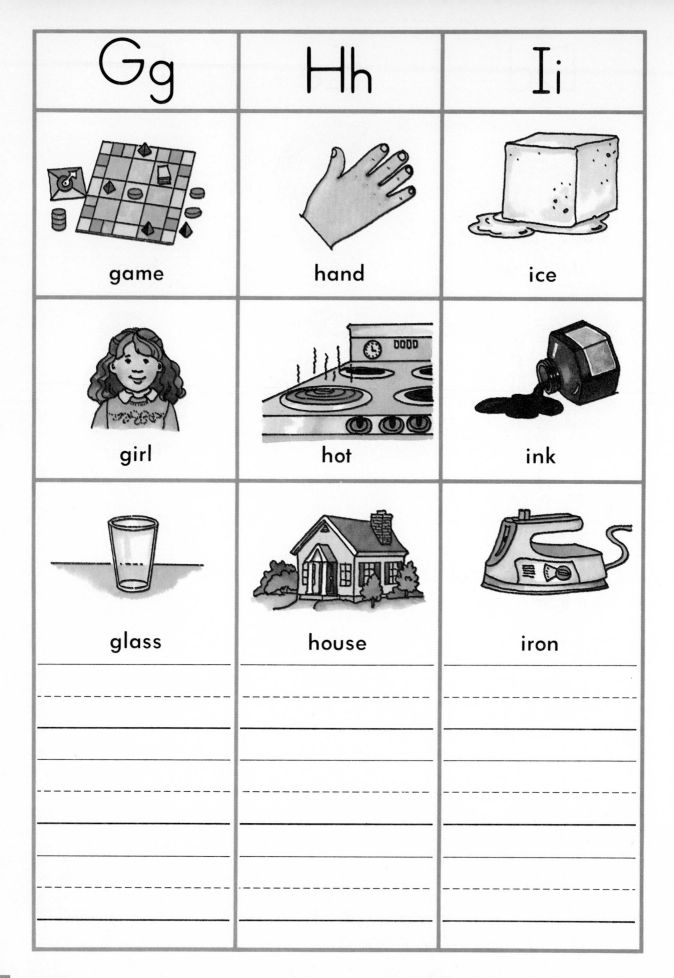

Gg	Hh	Ii
game	hand	ice
girl	hot	ink
glass	house	iron

Student's Handbook: Picture Dictionary

Children use the Picture Dictionary for spelling help and for dictionary lessons. Throughout the year, they add their own words on the lines provided.

Jj	Kk	Ll

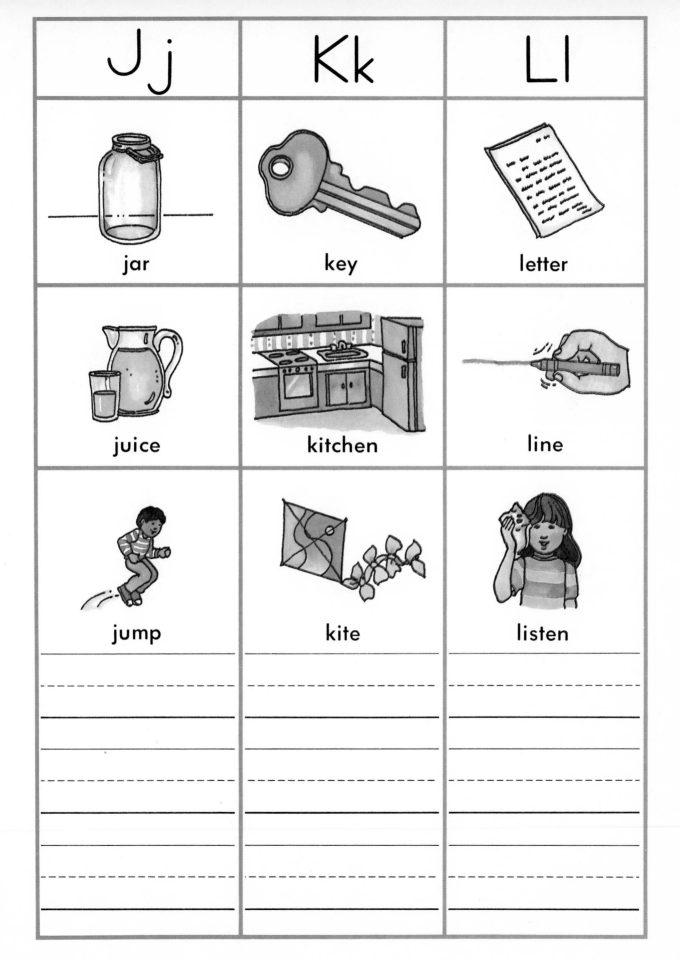

jar

key

letter

juice

kitchen

line

jump

kite

listen

Children use the Picture Dictionary for spelling help and for dictionary lessons. Throughout the year, they add their own words on the lines provided.

Student's Handbook: Picture Dictionary

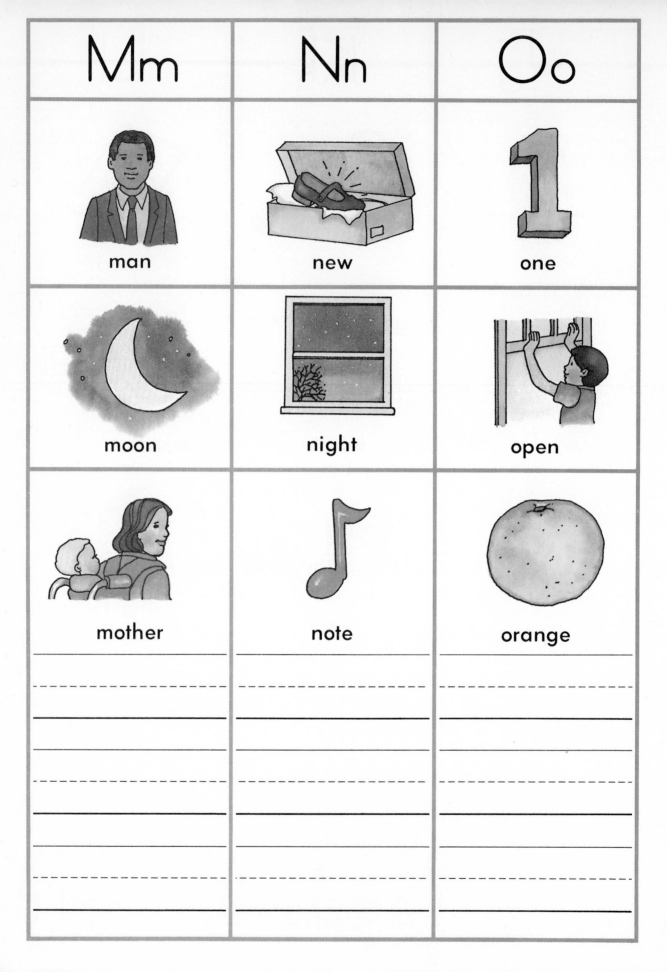

Mm	Nn	Oo
man	new	one
moon	night	open
mother	note	orange

Student's Handbook: Picture Dictionary

Children use the Picture Dictionary for spelling help and for dictionary lessons. Throughout the year, they add their own words on the lines provided.

Pp	Qq	Rr

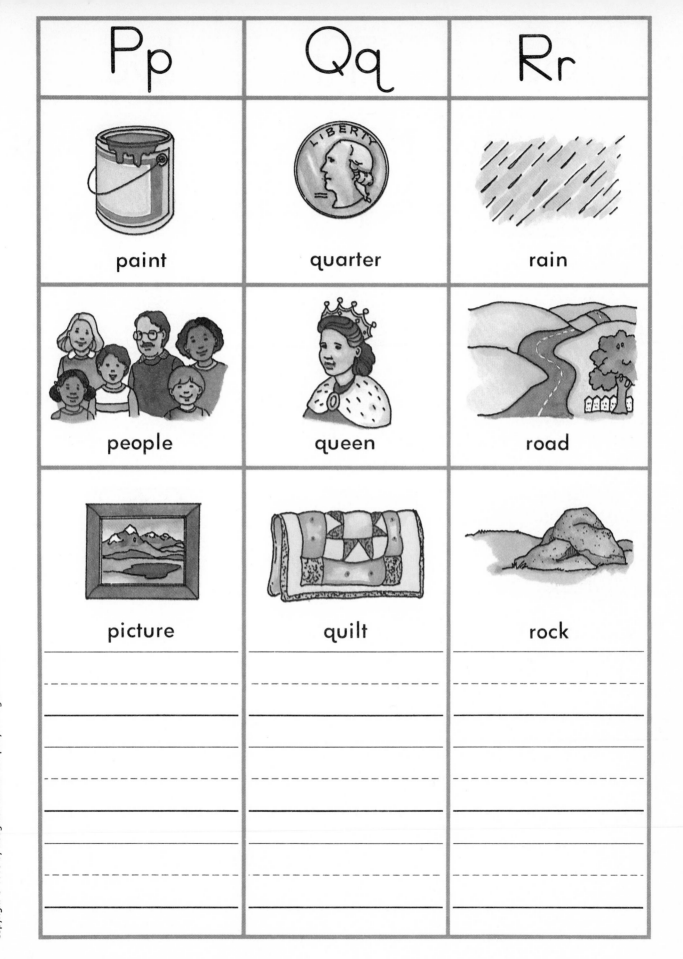

paint	quarter	rain
people	queen	road
picture	quilt	rock

Children use the Picture Dictionary for spelling help and for dictionary lessons. Throughout the year, they add their own words on the lines provided.

Student's Handbook: Picture Dictionary

251

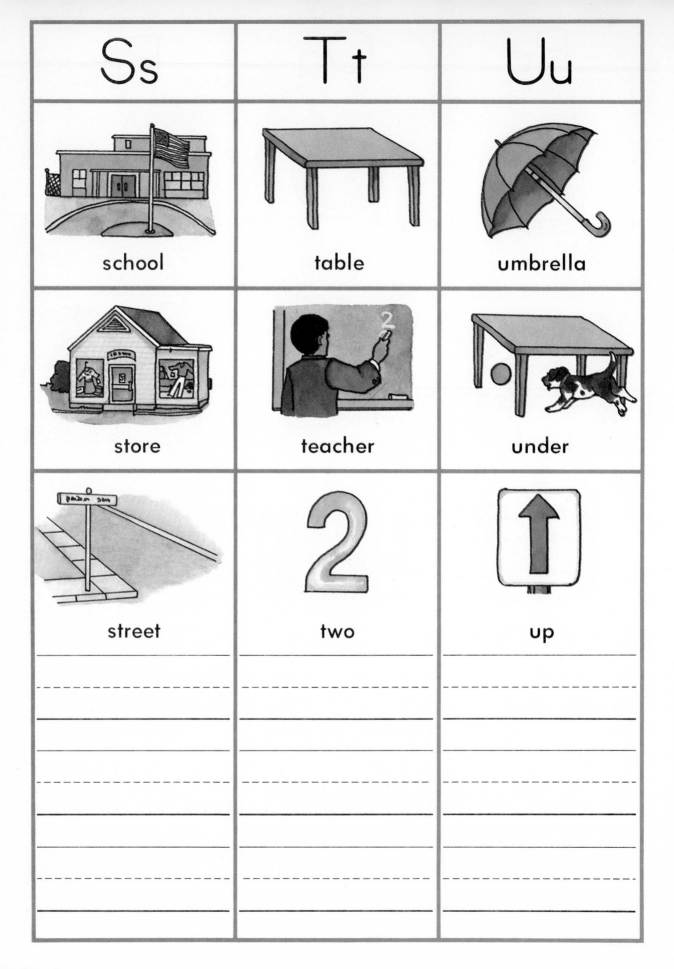

Ss	**Tt**	**Uu**
school	table	umbrella
store	teacher	under
street	two	up

Student's Handbook: Picture Dictionary

Children use the Picture Dictionary for spelling help and for dictionary lessons. Throughout the year, they add their own words on the lines provided.

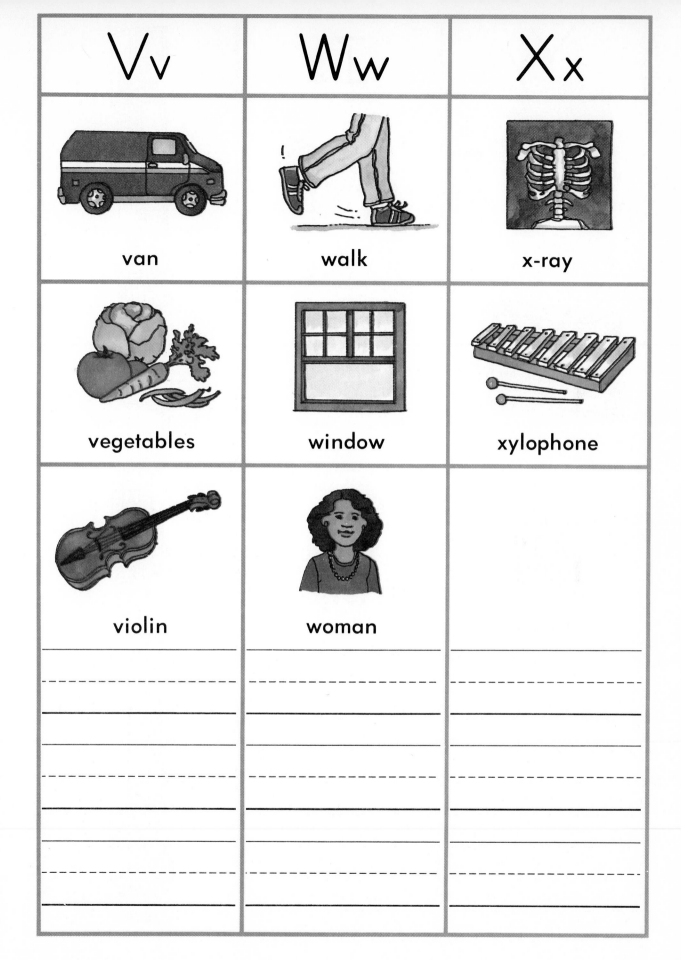

Vv	Ww	Xx
van	walk	x-ray
vegetables	window	xylophone
violin	woman	

Children use the Picture Dictionary for spelling help and for dictionary lessons. Throughout the year, they add their own words on the lines provided.

Student's Handbook: Picture Dictionary

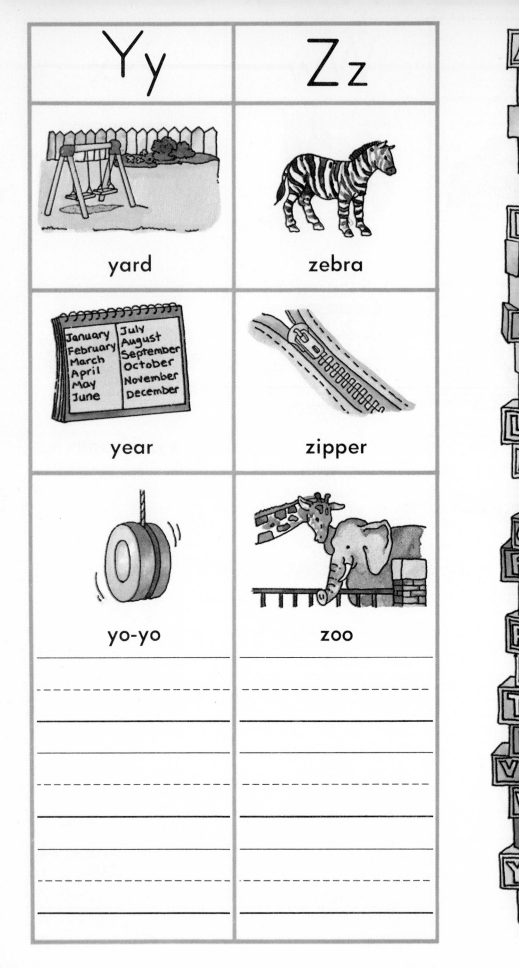

Yy	Zz
yard	zebra
year	zipper
yo-yo	zoo

Children use the Picture Dictionary for spelling help and for dictionary lessons. Throughout the year, they add their own words on the lines provided.

■ INDEX ■

Numbers in **bold type** indicate pages where skills are taught. Names in italics refer to the punchouts at the back of the pupil book.

Abbreviations, 141
Addresses, 141
Adjectives
  comparative and superlative forms of, **221–222, 225, 233**
  recognizing and using, **215,** 216–220, 224–225, 227–232, *Describing Word Game*
  writing in sentences, 219, 224, 231
Agreement, subject-verb, 191–194, 197–200, 205, 208–209, 211–212
Alliteration, 173
Alphabetical order
  letters in, **59–60,** 61–64
  words in, **241**
  words in a dictionary, **242,** 243–254
Antonyms, 81, *Opposites Game*
Apostrophes, 201, 213
Art, as a response to storytelling, 20, 26, 177, 238
Audience, 132, 135, 179
Author, 236

be, **forms of, 193–194,** 199–200, 205, 209, 212
Beginning, middle, end, of a story, 177
Book reports, 237–239
Bottom, 44

Capitalization
  forming capital letters, **59–60,** 61–62, 63
  of book titles, 237–239
  of days of the week, **153,** 159, 168
  of first word of sentence, **105,** 108, 113–115, 119, 122
  of months, **154,** 159, 169
  of names, **151–152,** 158–159, 167
  of pronoun *I,* **80,** 83, 93, 111, 125
Characters, storybook, 35
Class story, 97–101
Classifying, 51–52

Color recognition, 41–42
Commas
  after greeting and closing in letter, 129–131, 134–137
  with dates, 130
Communication, nonverbal, 28
Comparison, degrees of, 221–222, 225, 233
Composition
  models, 101, 128, 129, 130, 141, 237
  modes
    expressive, 131, 132–141
    narrative, 97–101, 178–187
  skills, 129–131, 177
  steps in writing. *See* Writing process
  types of
    letters, 129–141
    stories, 97–101, 178–187
Compound words, 157
Conferences, about writing, 100, 136, 182
Contractions, 201, 213
Creative writing, 97–101, 178–187

Dates, 130
Days of the week, **153,** 158–159, 168
Descriptions, 71, 220, 224
Details, 11–15, 19–20, 31–36
Dictionary, 242–243. *See also* Picture Dictionary
Directions. *See* Instructions
Discussions
  about pictures, 19, 25, **27,** 47, 98, 177
  about topic ideas, 98, 178–179
  about writing, 100, 136, 182
down, **43**

Editing. *See* Proofreading; Revising
End marks, **106, 108,** 110, 113–114, 116, 120–122, 124
Endings, inflectional, 195–196, 205
Envelopes, addressing, 141
Exact words, 203, 220, 232

Facts, 11–15, 31–36
First draft, 99, 134–135, 180–181
Friendly letters, 128, **129,** 132–141

Handwriting
  tracing and writing letters, **55–60,** 57–58, 61–63
  tracing and writing numbers, **65–66,** 69

  writing periods, **106,** 120
  writing question marks, **108,** 122
  writing apostrophes, **201,** 213
Homographs, 223
Homophones, 112

I, **80,** 83, 93, 111, 125
in, **43**
Indenting, 99, 101, 134, 136–137
Instructions, following, 39–40, 41–45, 53
Invitations, 129–131
is, are, **193**

Left and right, 45
Letters
  skills in writing, 129–131
  types
    friendly letter, 128, **129**
    invitation, **129–131**
    thank-you, **129**
  the writing process and, 132–141
Library, 235
Life skill, 29
Listening
  for colors, **41,** *Color Game*
  for details, **19–20**
  to follow directions, **39–40**
  for information, **29**
  to a poem, 95, 127, 173, 174
  for positional words, **43–45**
  for rhyme, 21, *Rhyme Game*
  for sequence, **22–24**
  to a story, 19–20, 22–24, 96, 128, 175–176
Literary terms
  author, 236
  rhyme, **21**
  title, **236,** 237–239
Literature
  responding to, 19–24, 236, 238–239
  types of
    fable
      "The Lion and the Mouse," 175–176
    fiction
      "The Bear's Toothache," 19–20
      "The Forgetful Bears," 236
      "The Letter," 128
      "Lost in the Museum," 96
      "Mike Mulligan and His Steam Shovel," 22–24

256

My Book About Me

By _____

My Book of Favorites

By _____

Unit 3: My Book of Favorites

My Story

By _____

Unit 11: Story